Dedicated to curious minds and little hearts.
May the pages of this coloring book open the
doors to a world of wonder and discovery.
Through the beautiful illustrations of God's
stories, you can find inspiration, joy, and a
deeper connection to the timeless teachings
of the Bible.
With love and blessings,

AWS
01/2024

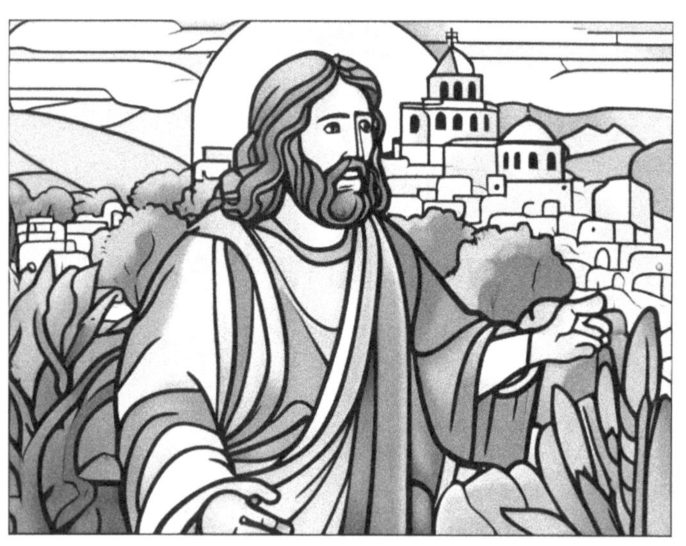 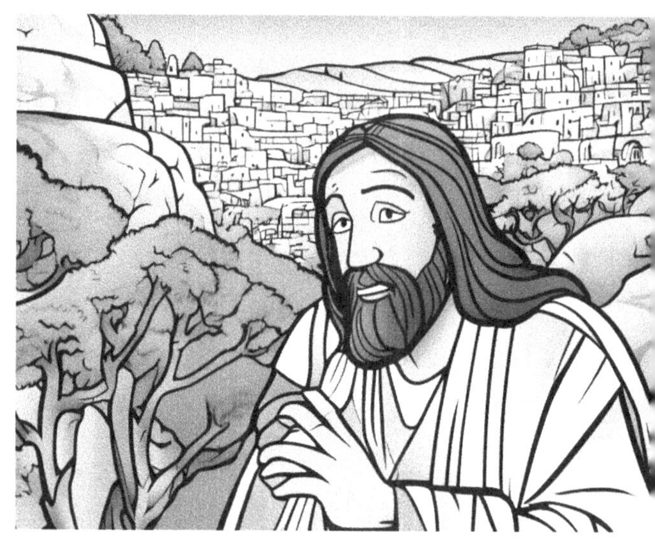

THE BOOK BELONGS TO:

____

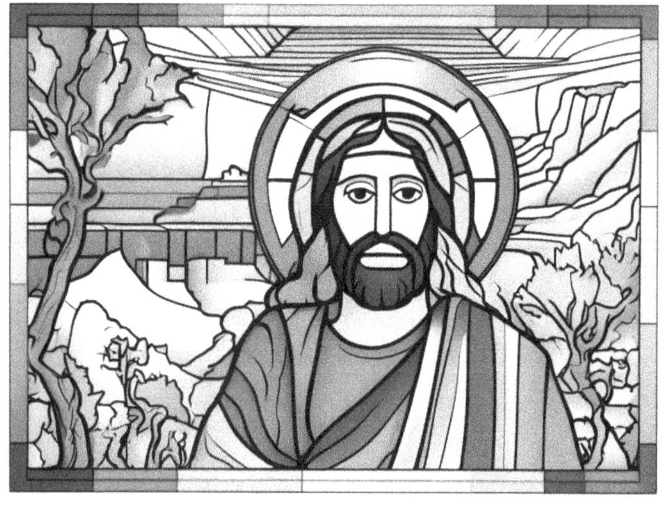 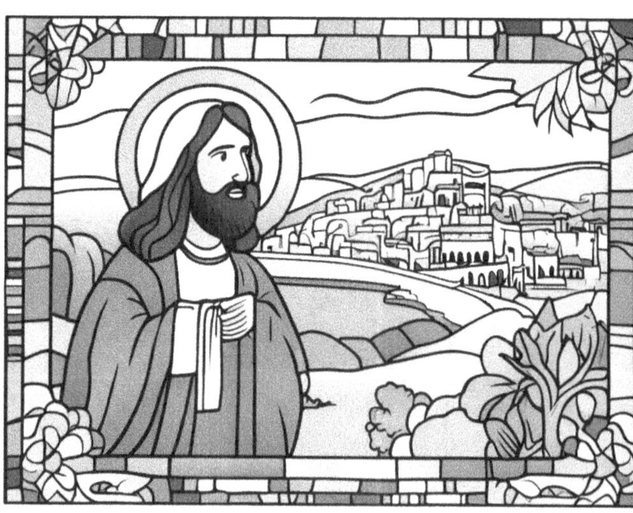

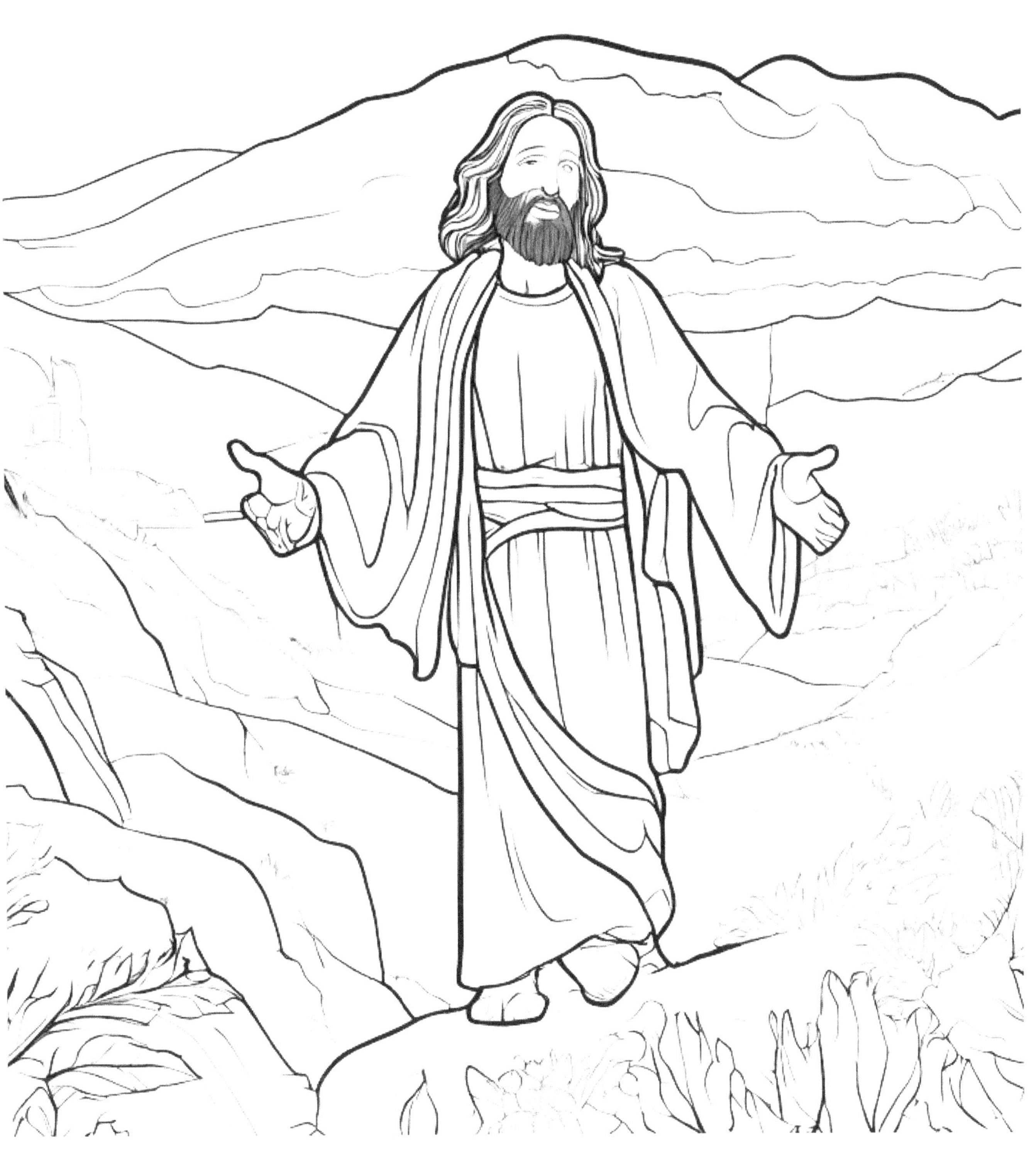

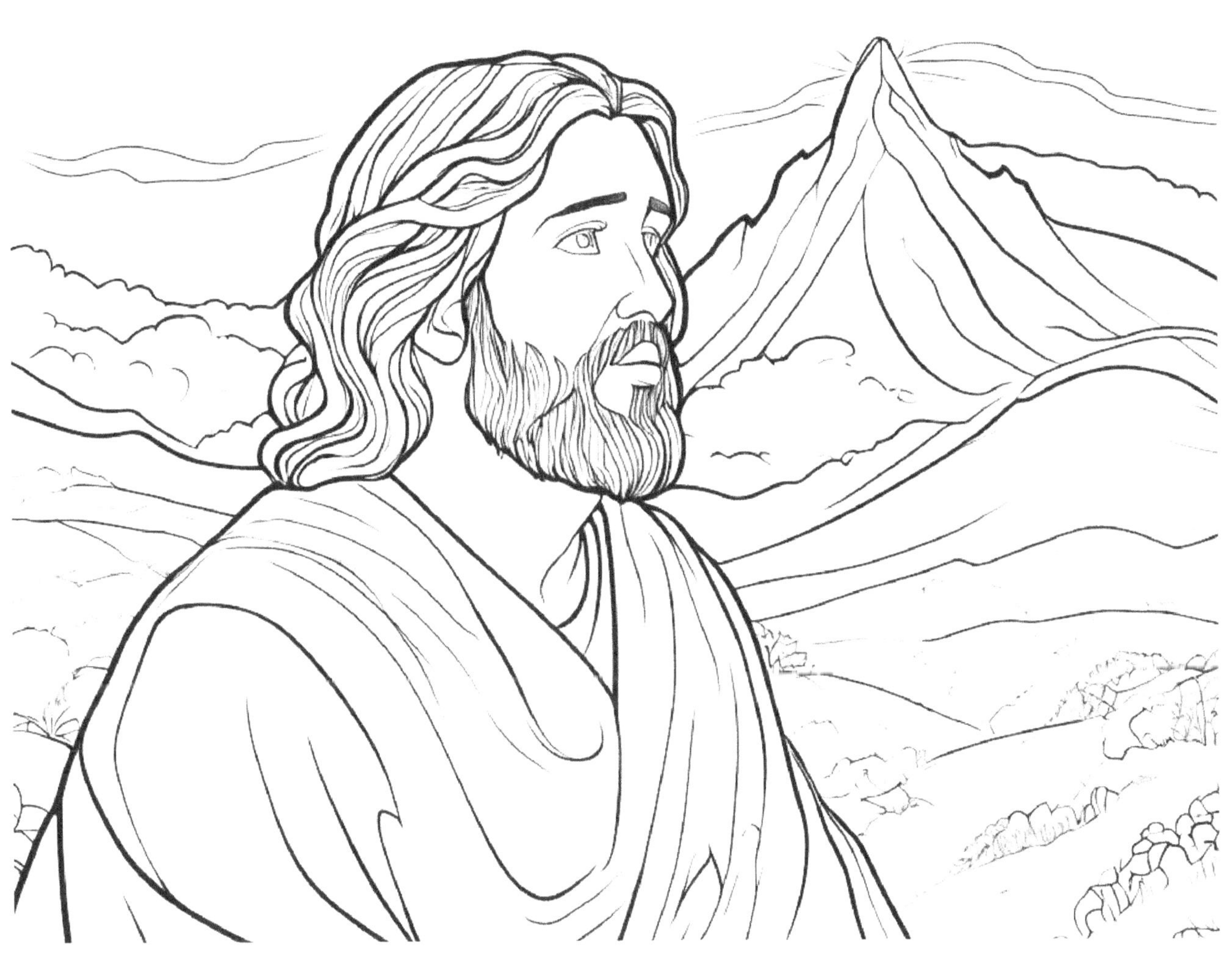

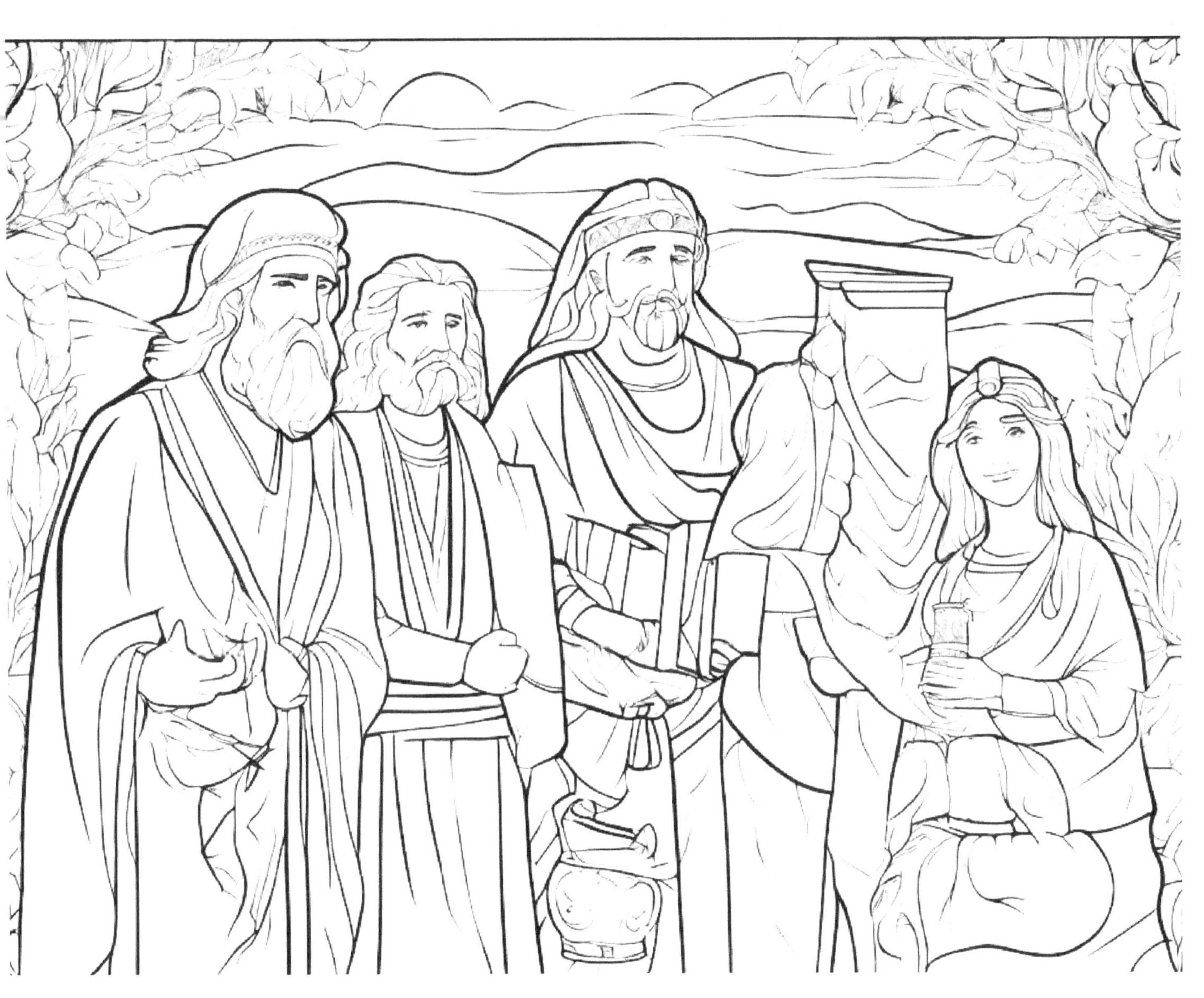

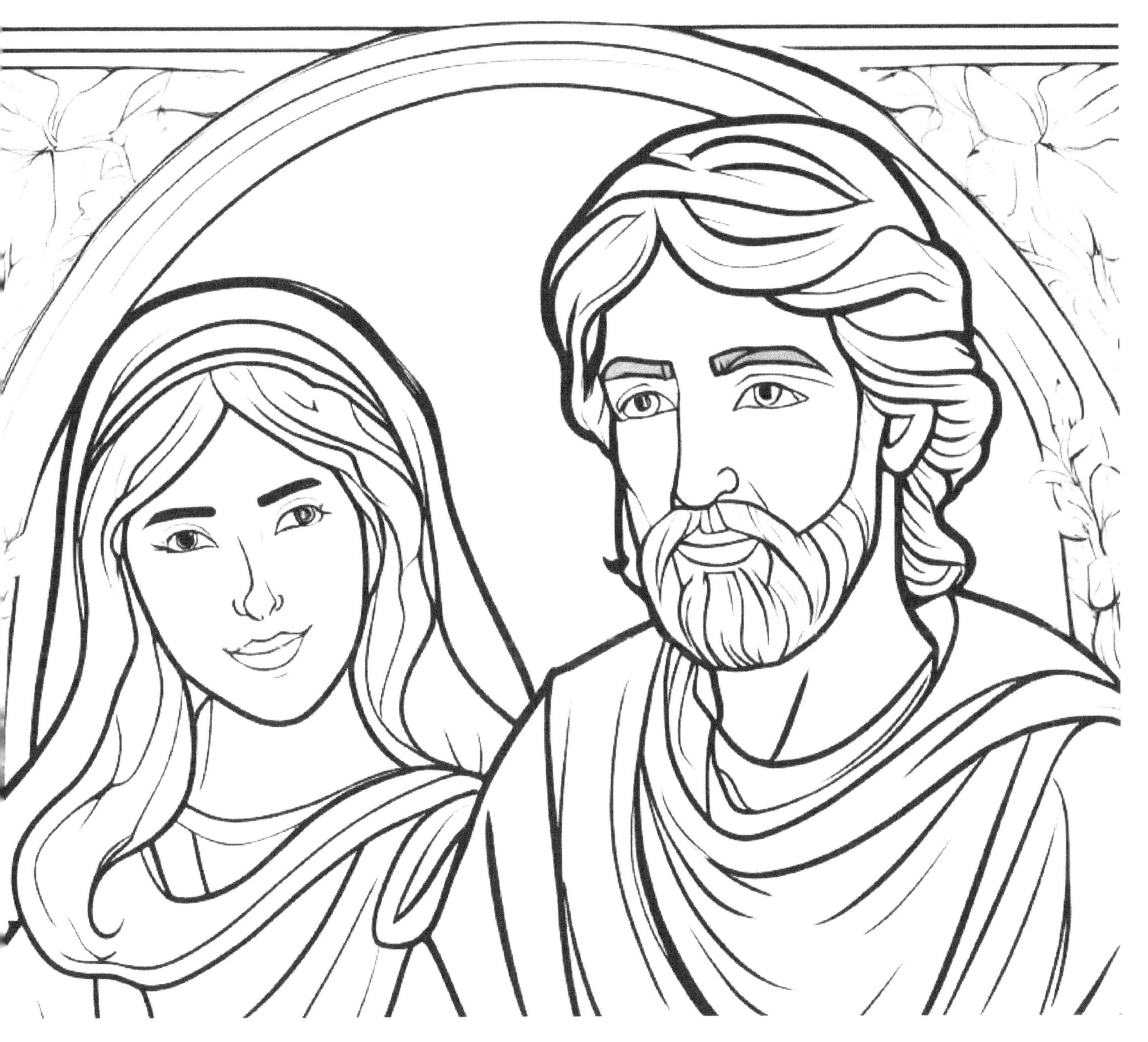

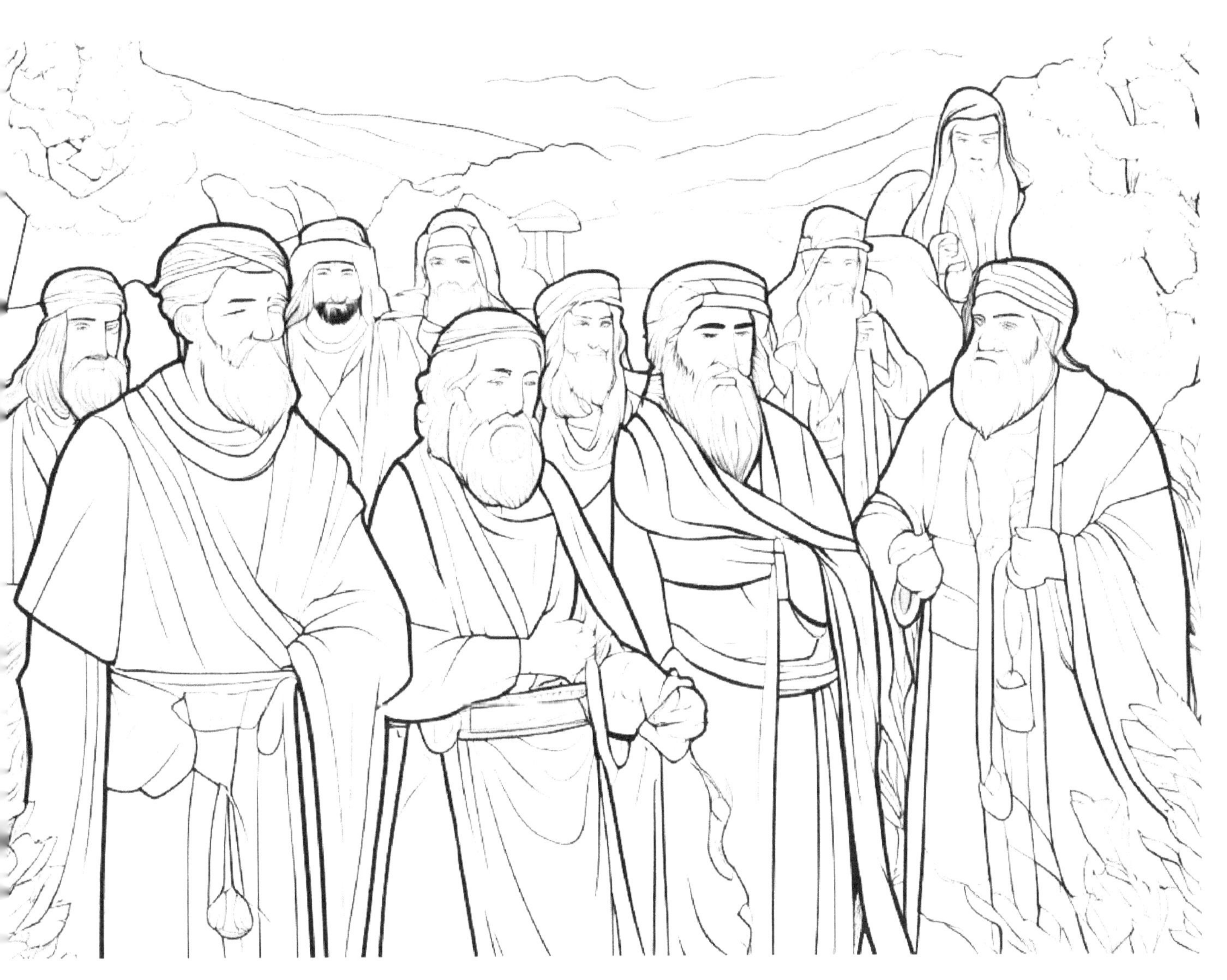

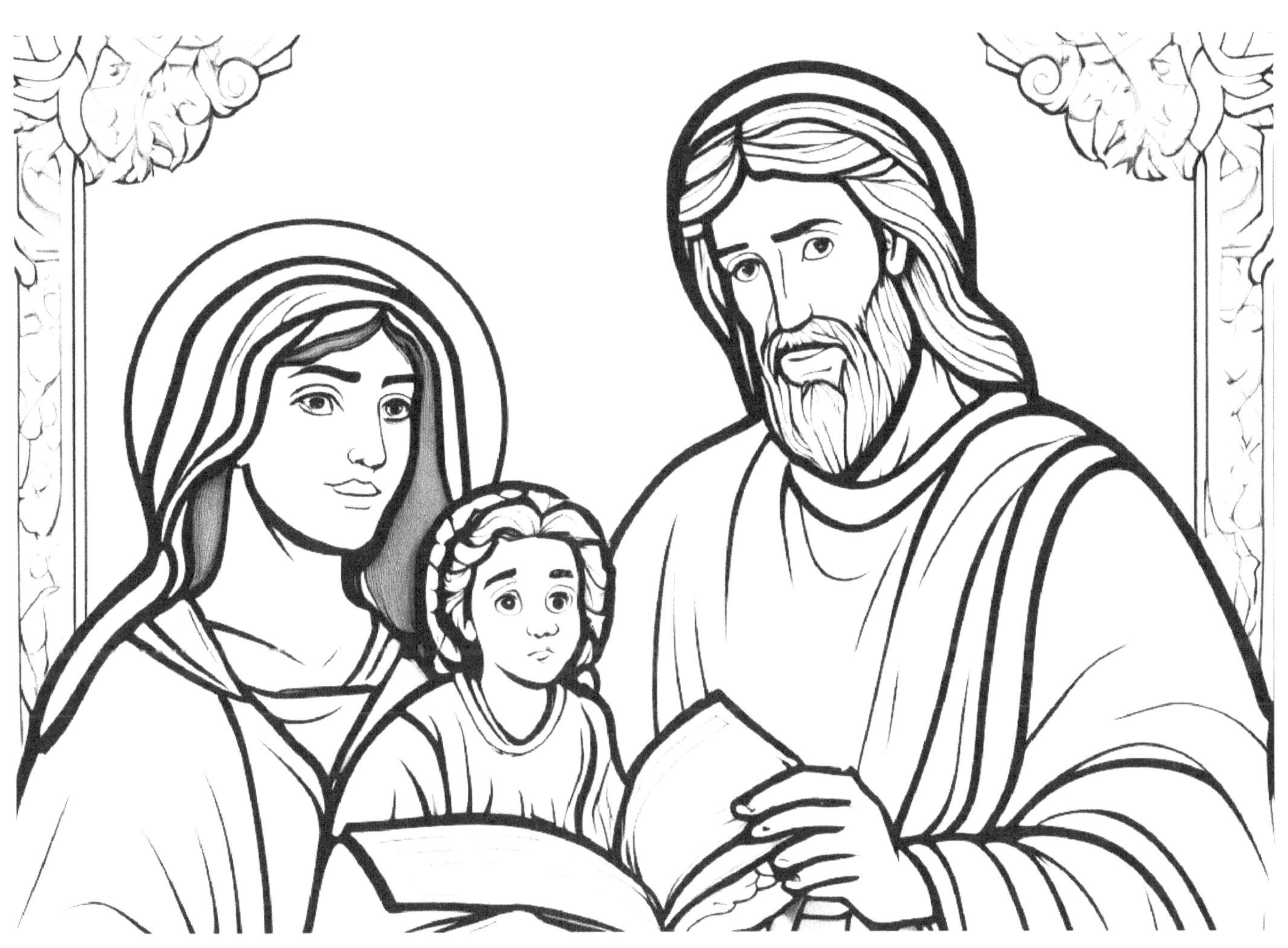

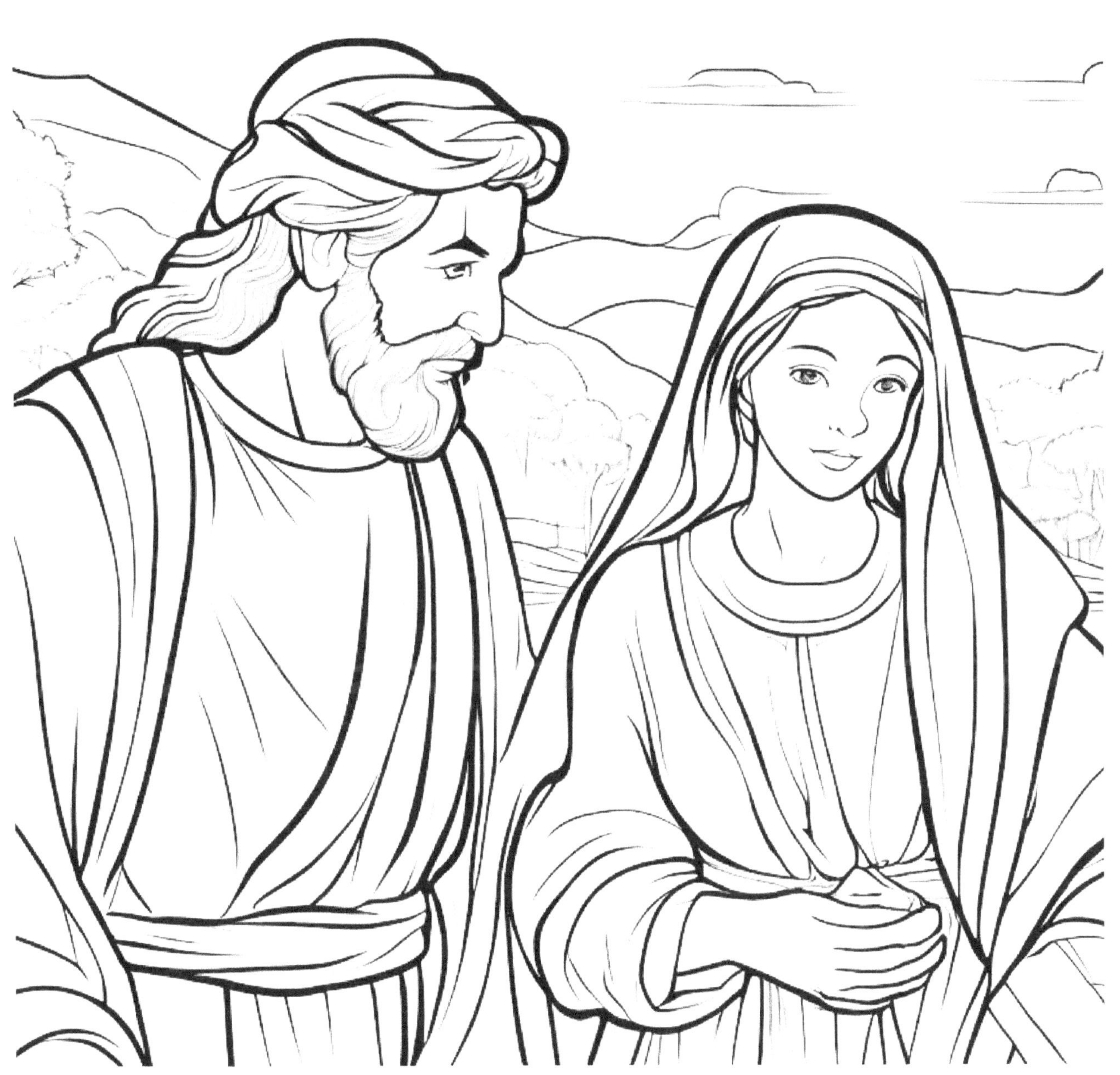

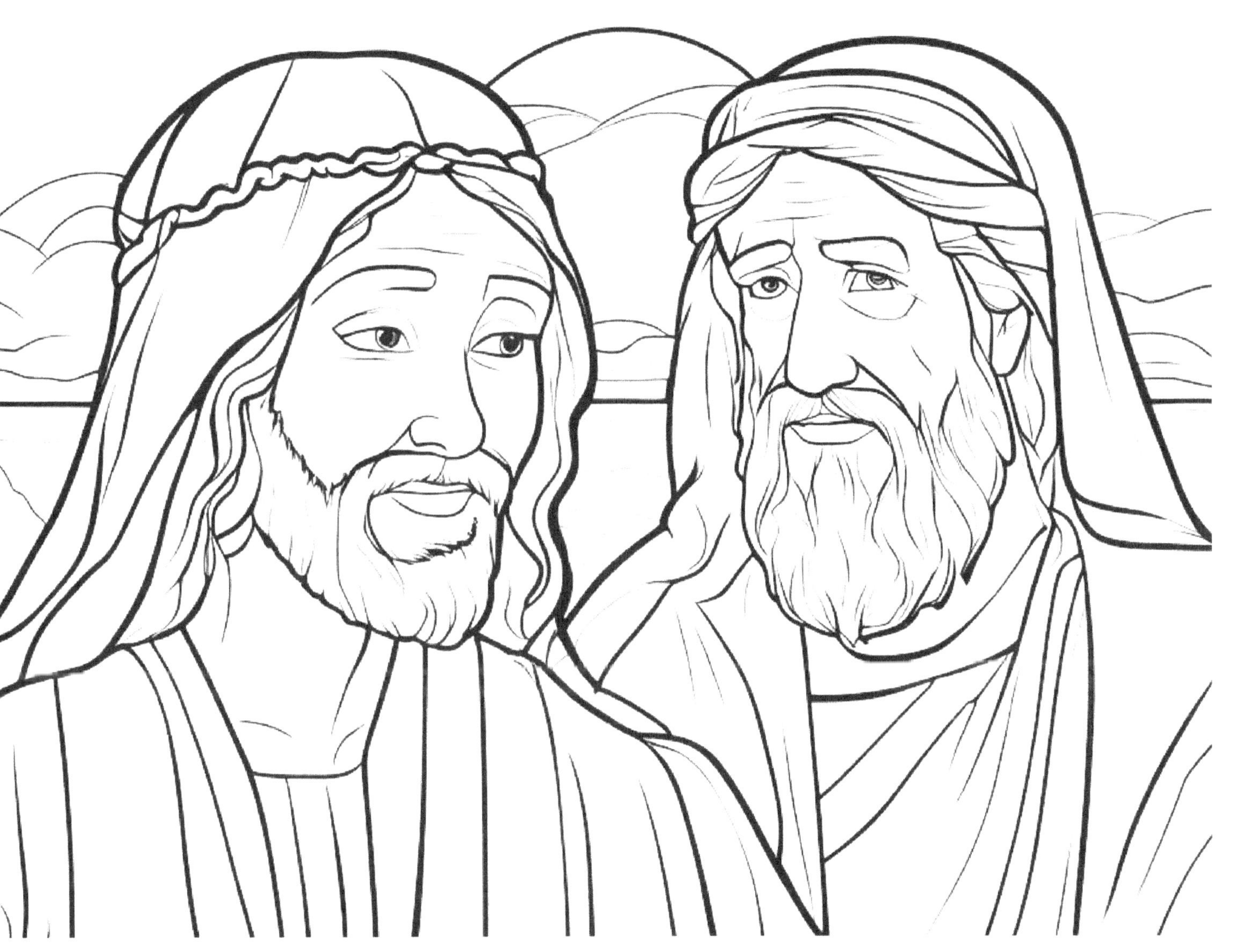

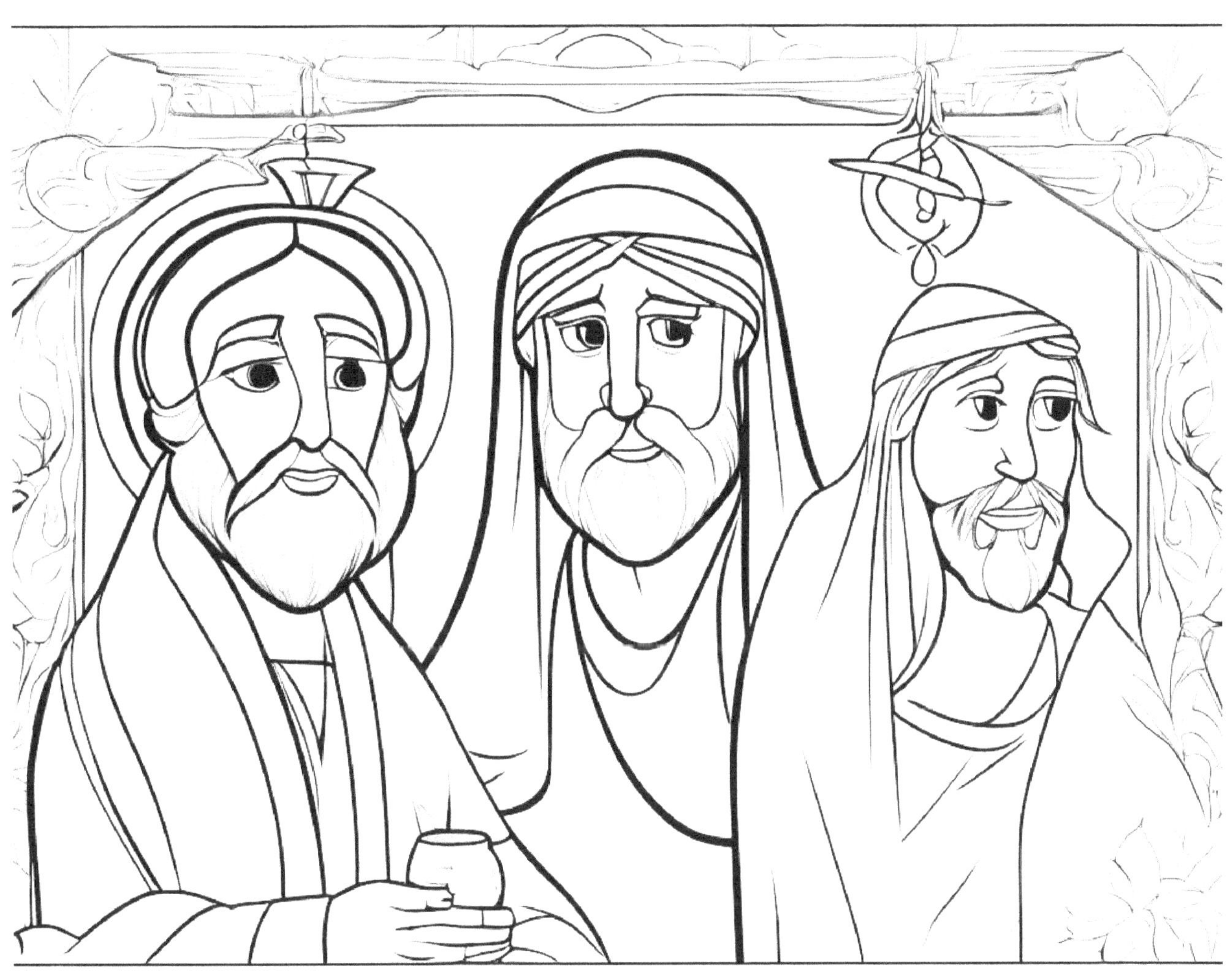

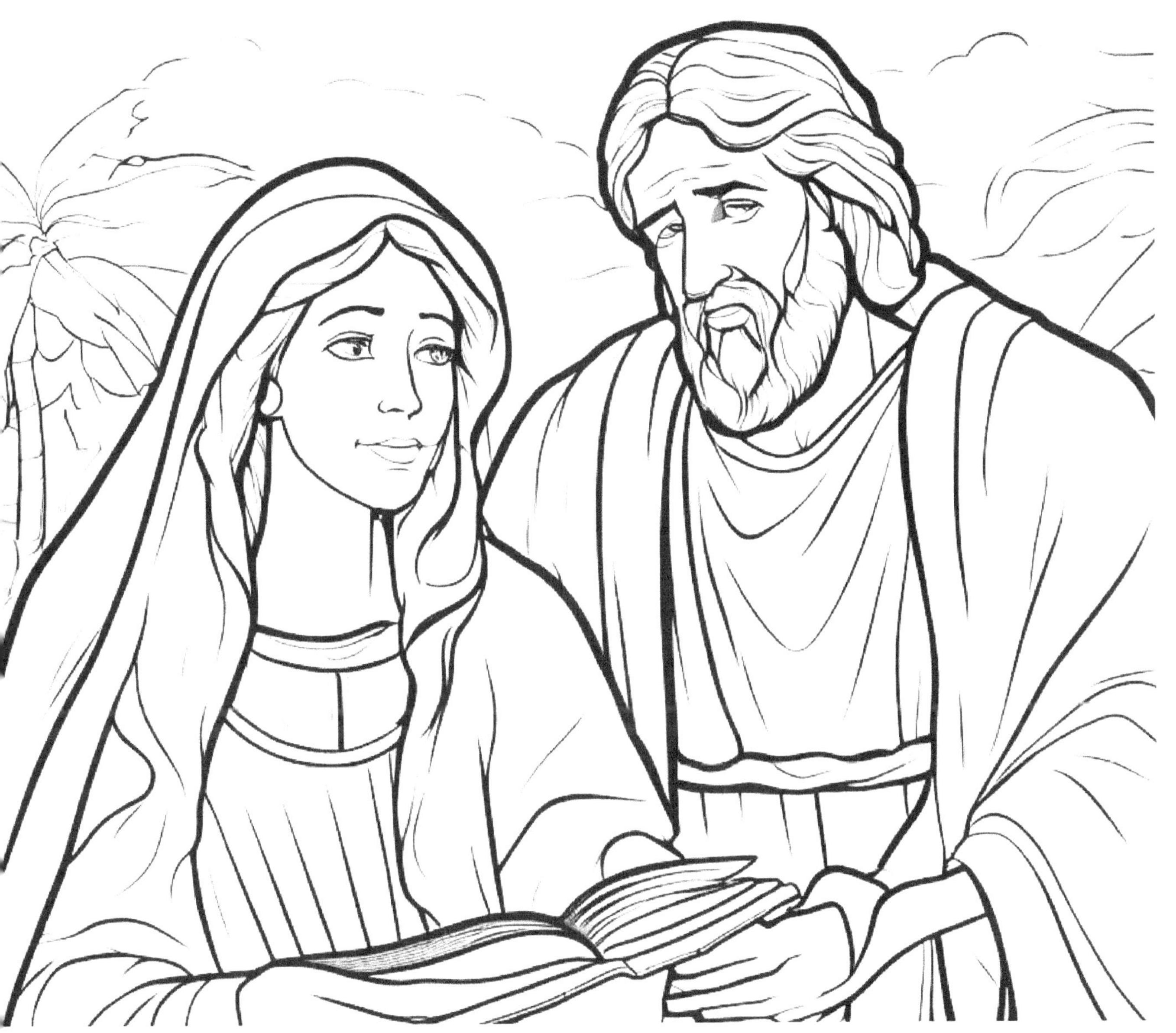

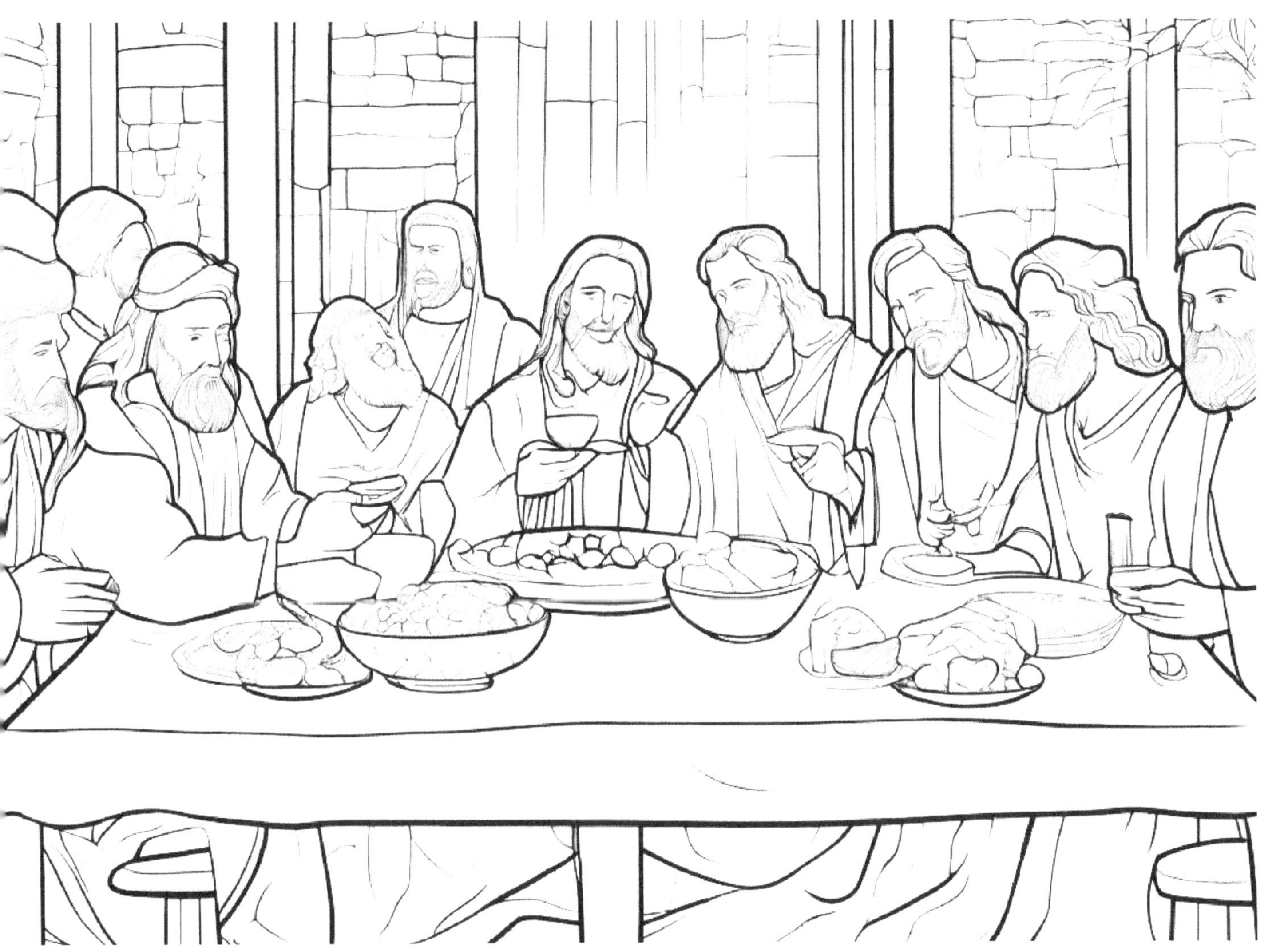

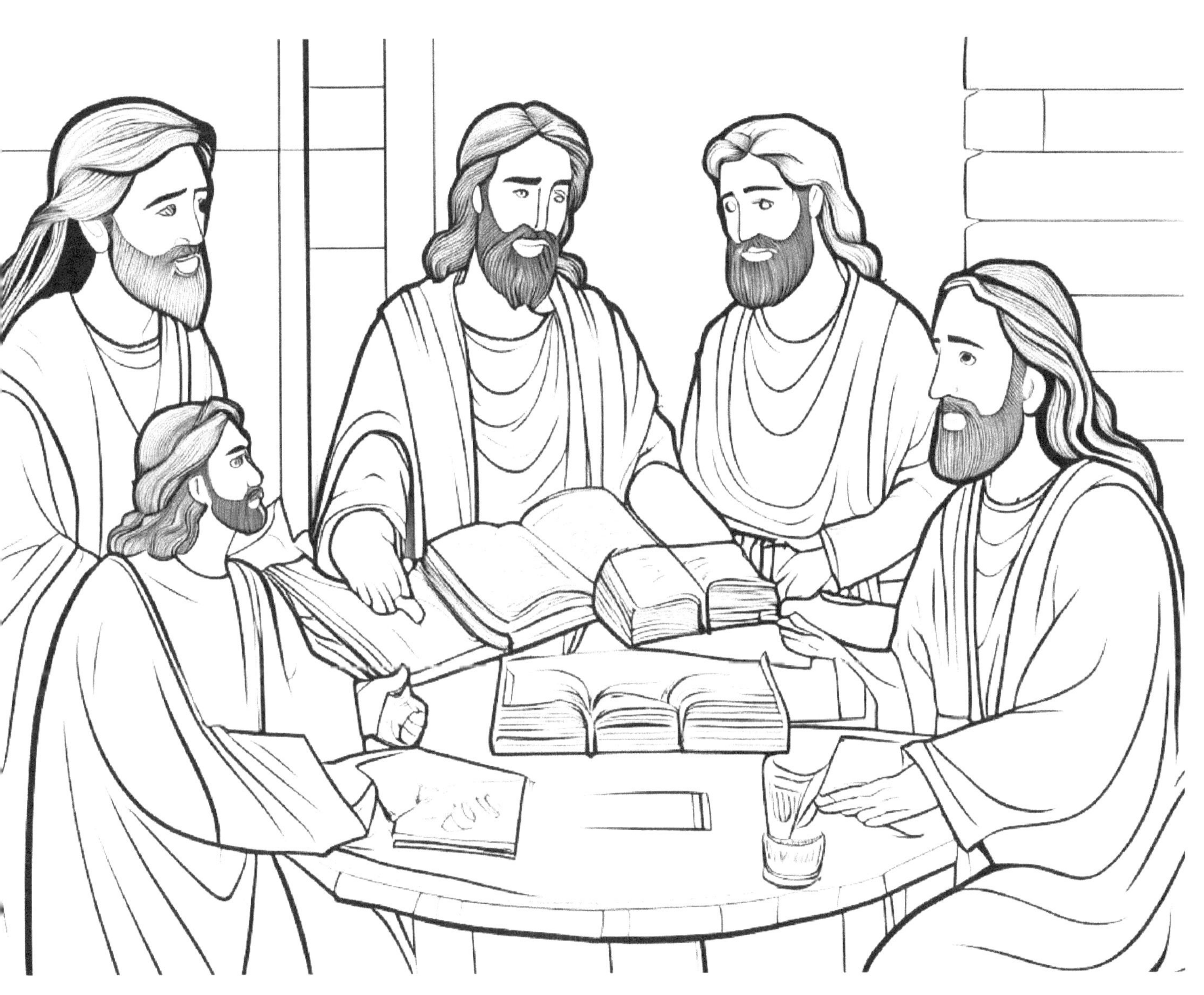

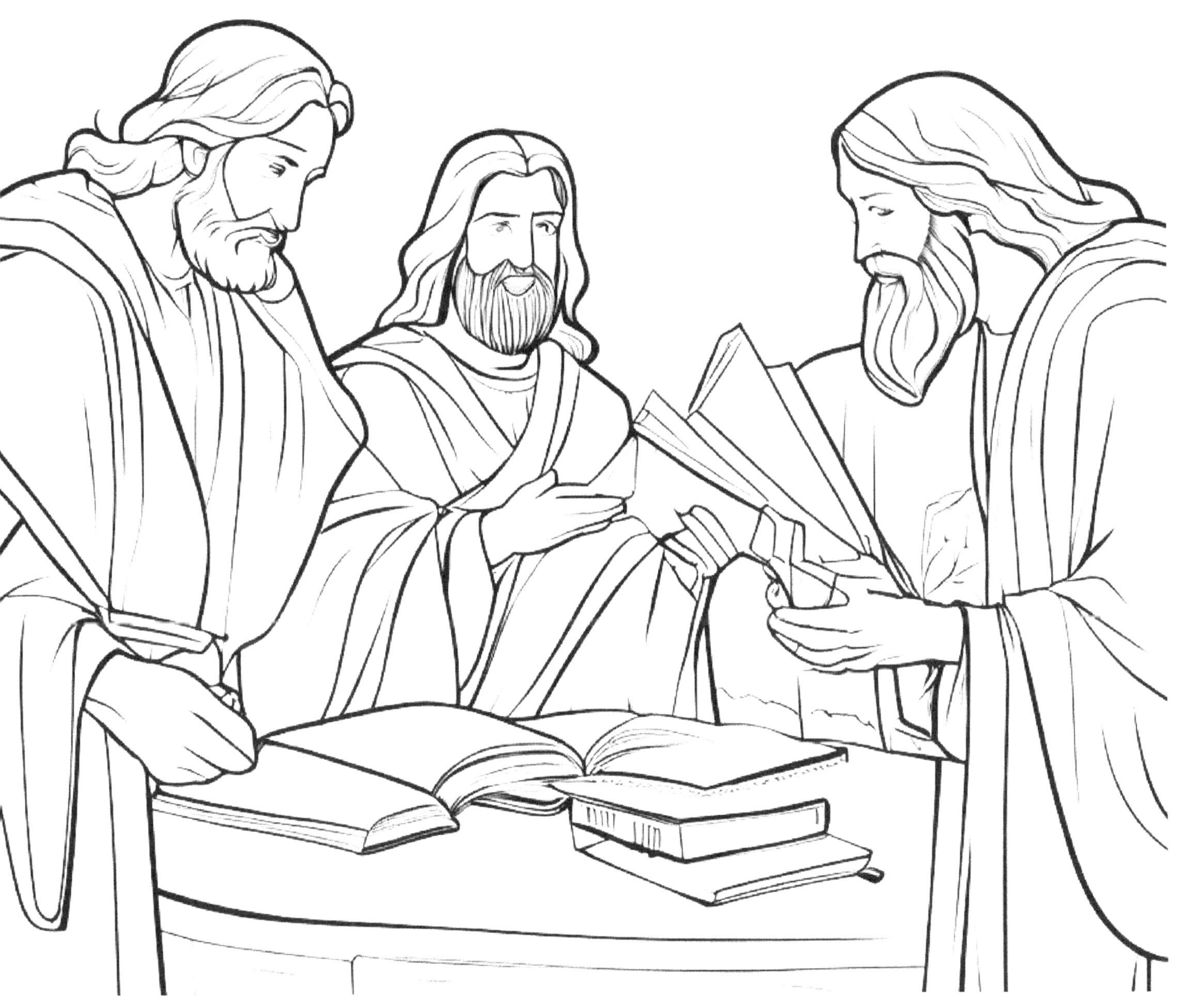

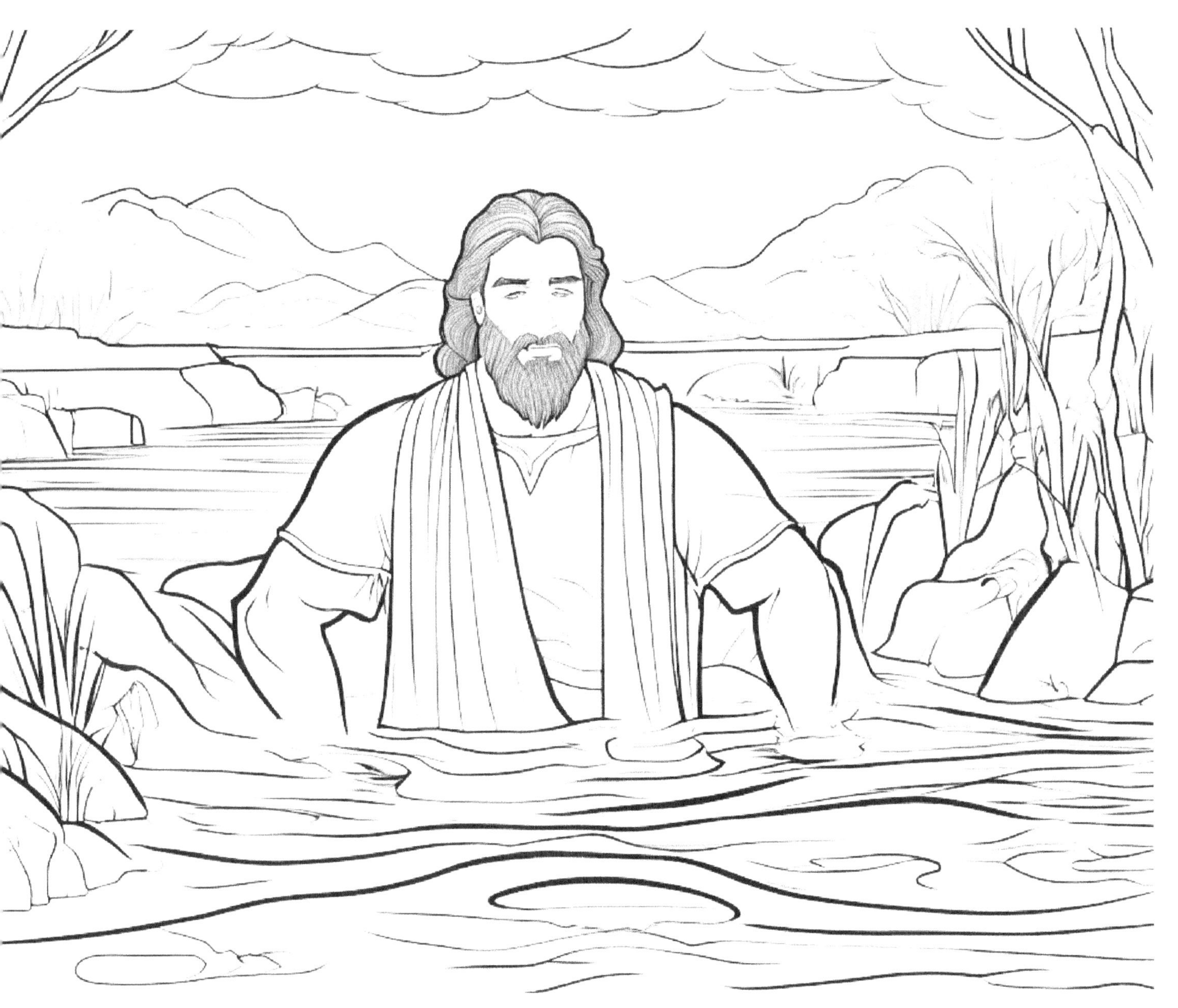

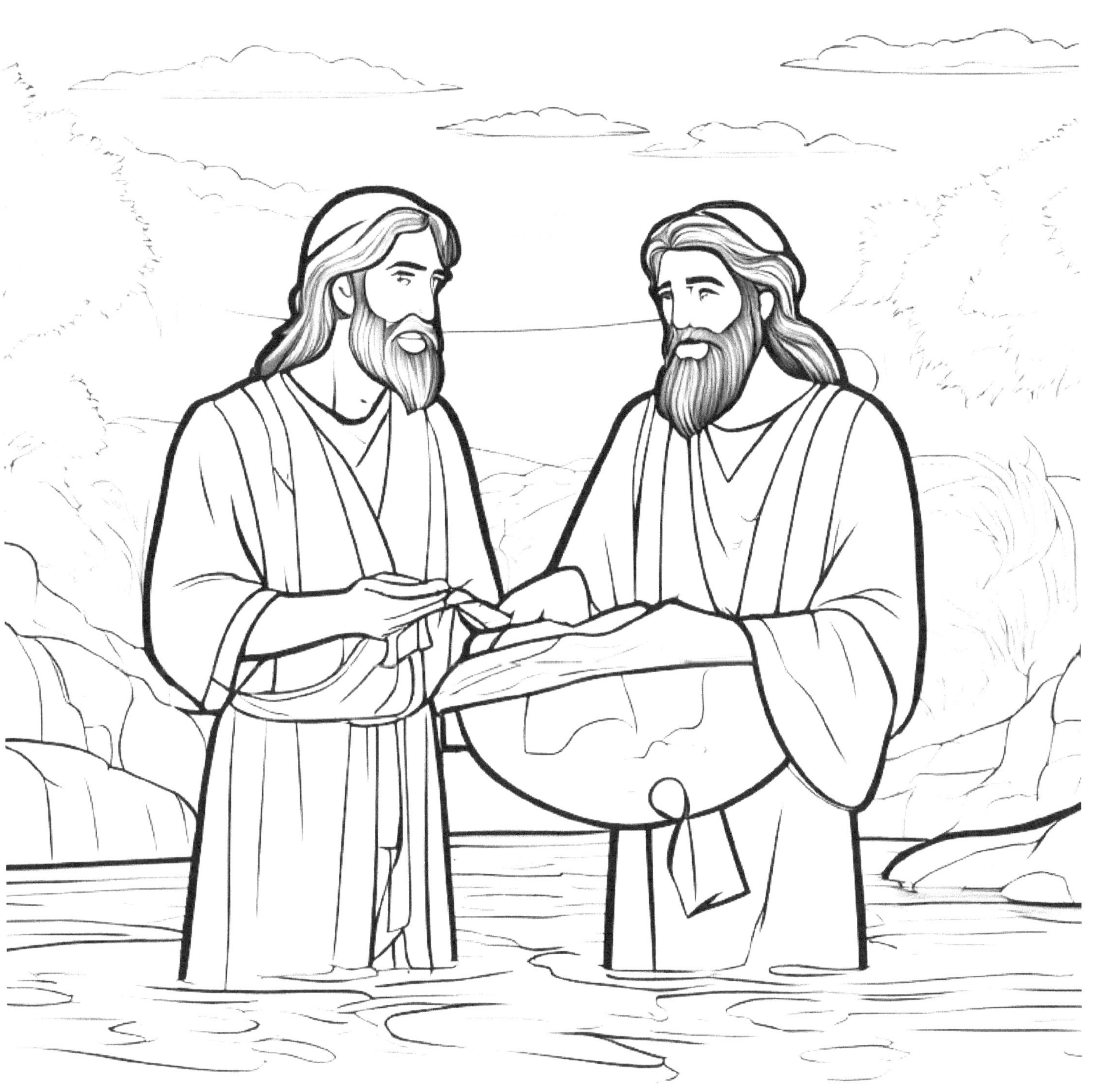

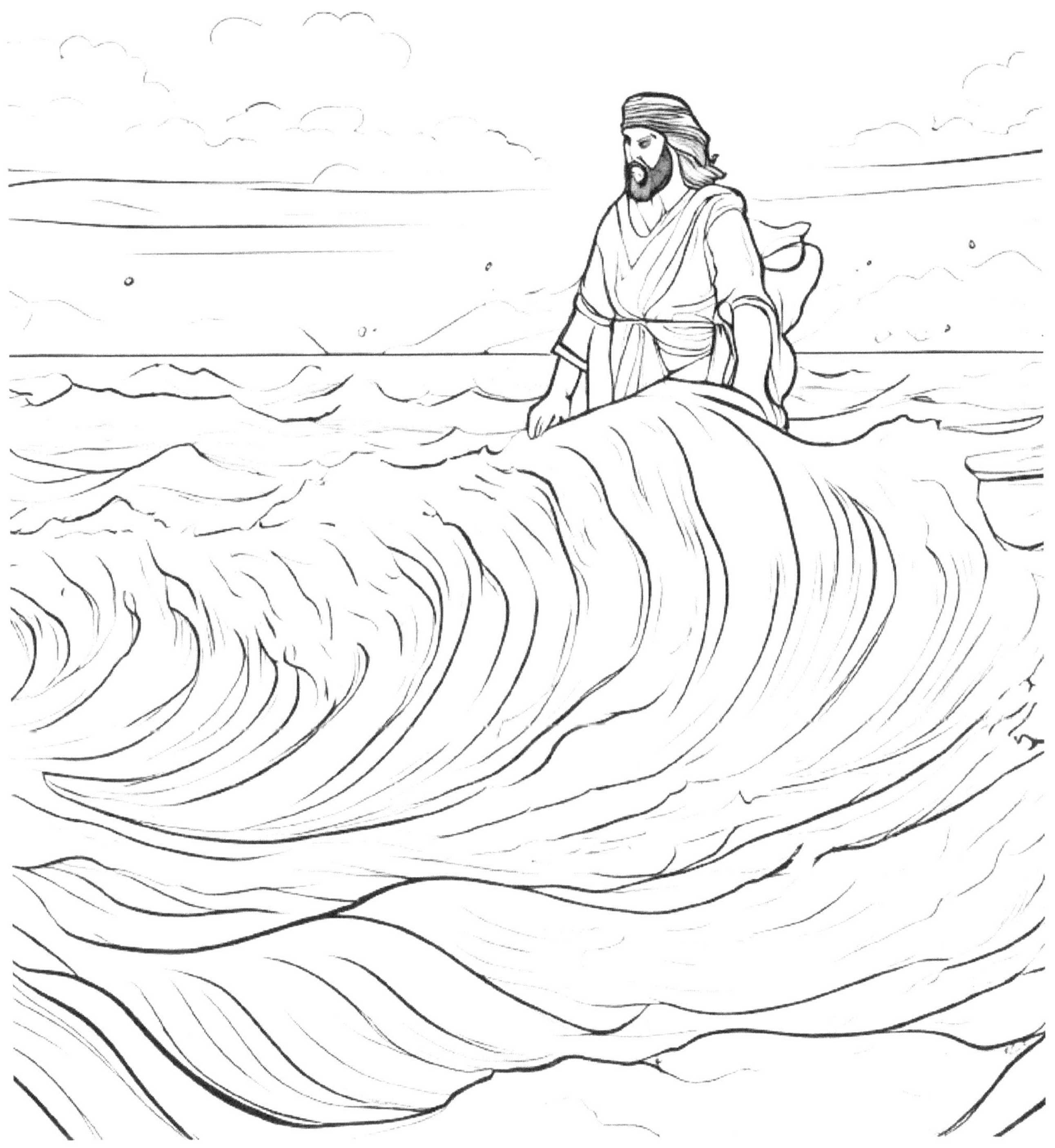

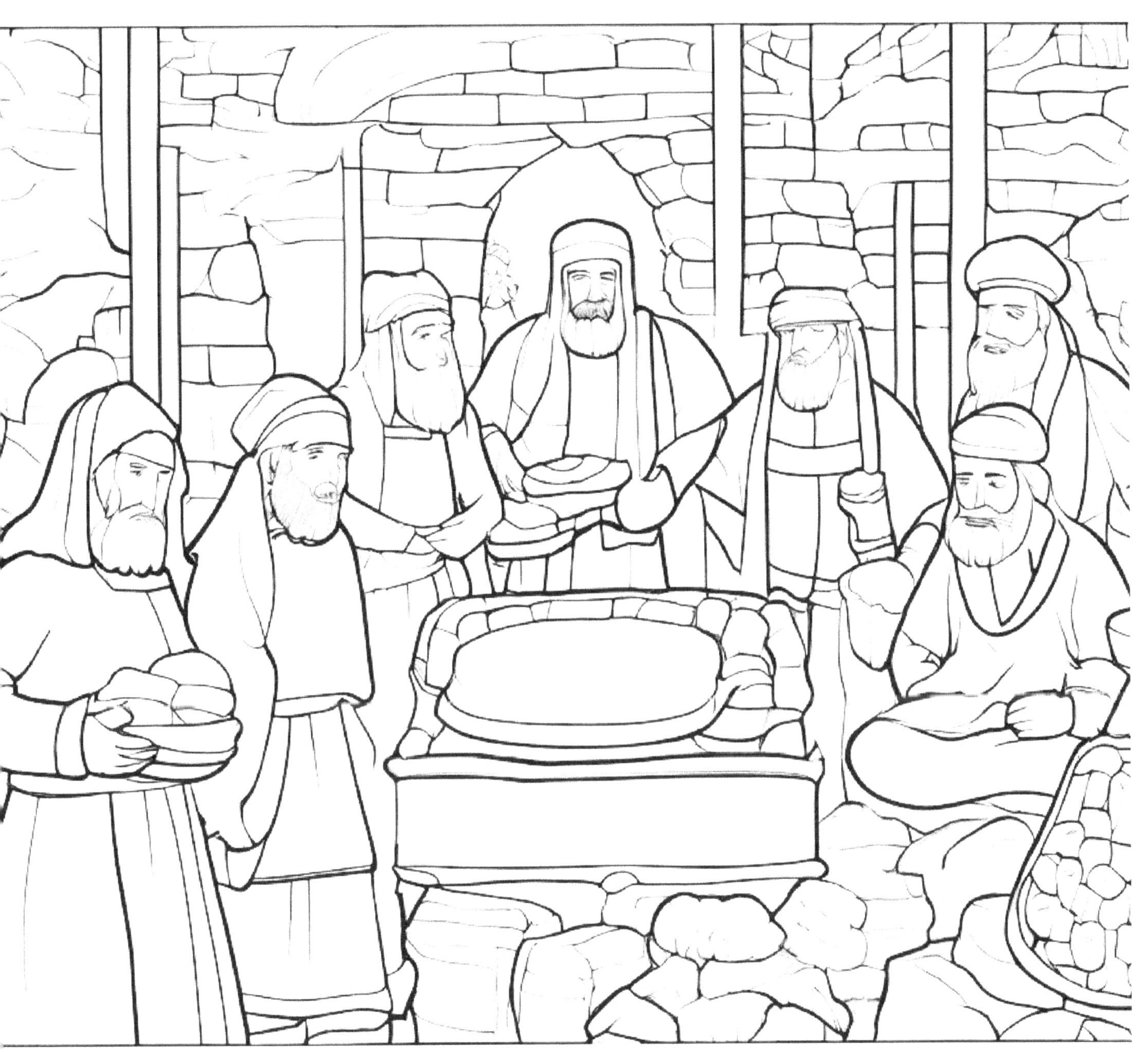

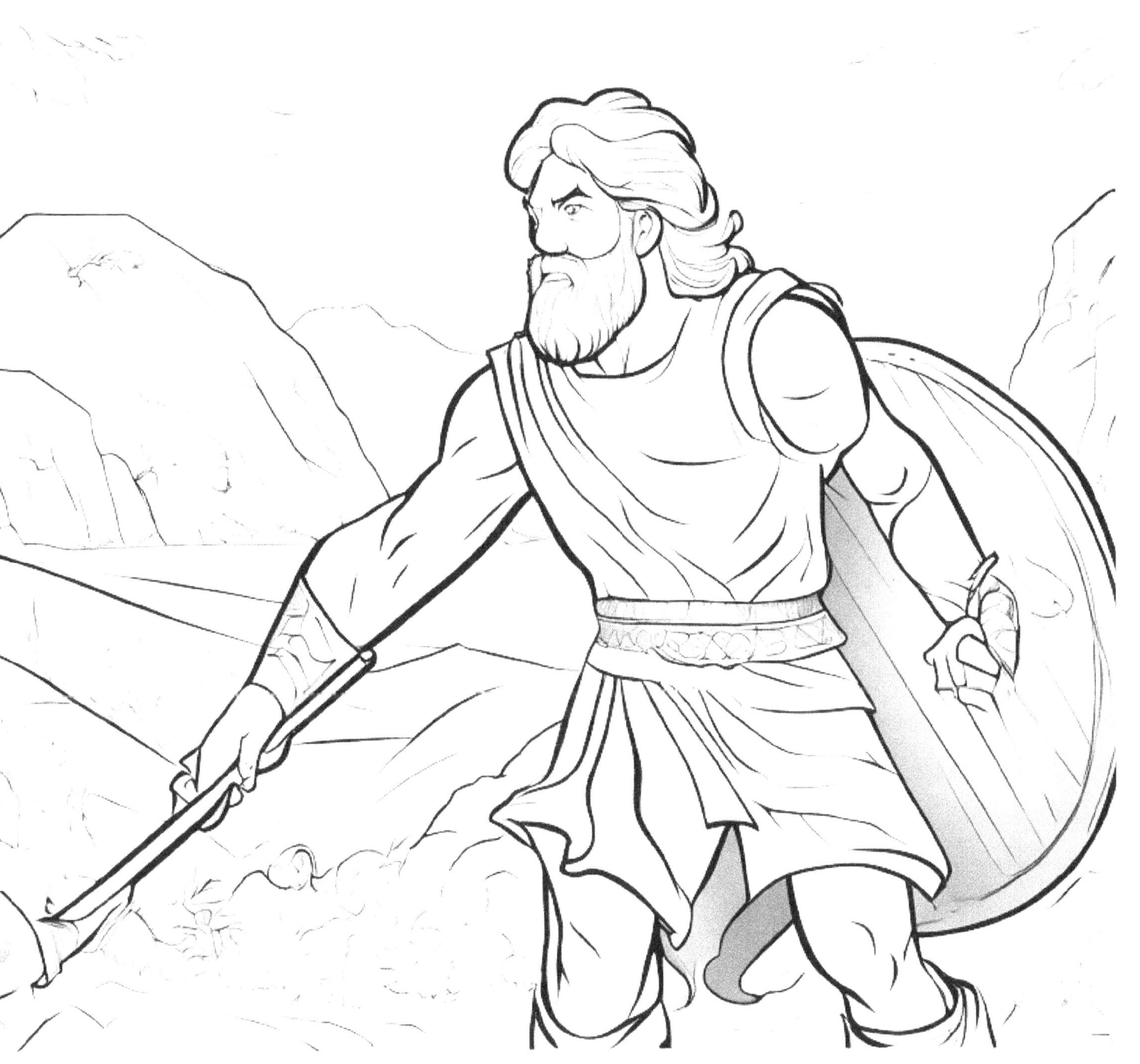

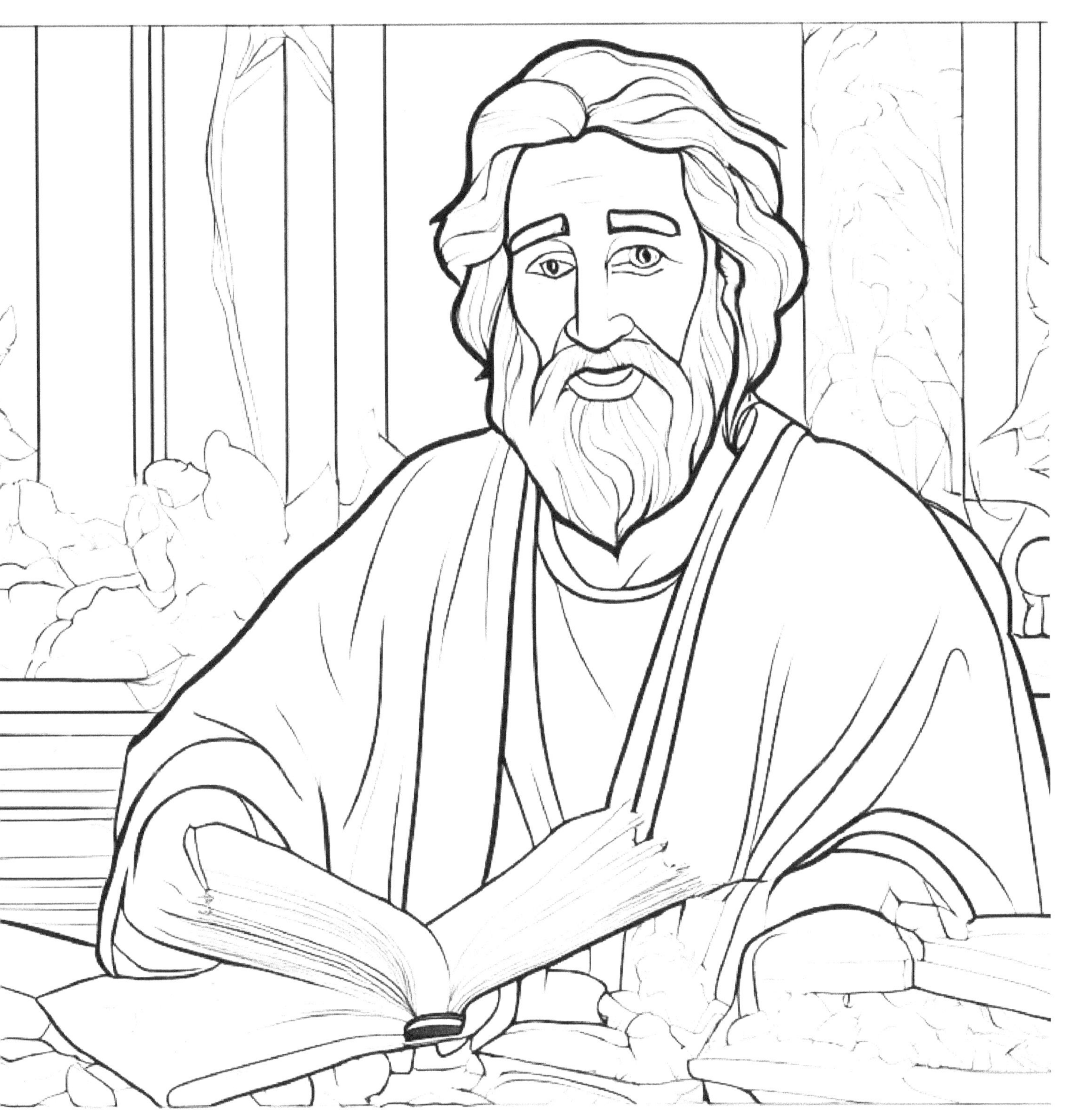

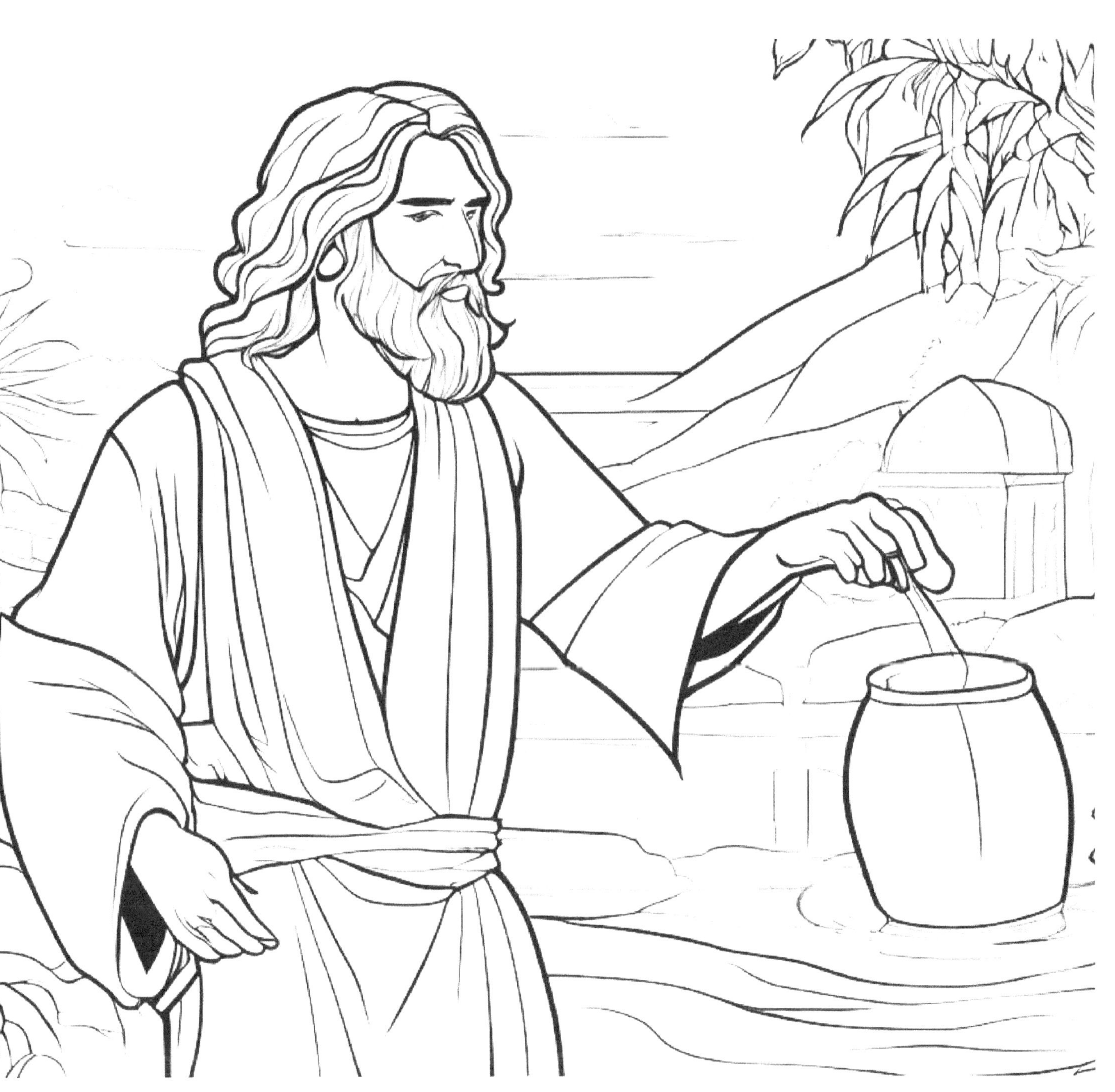

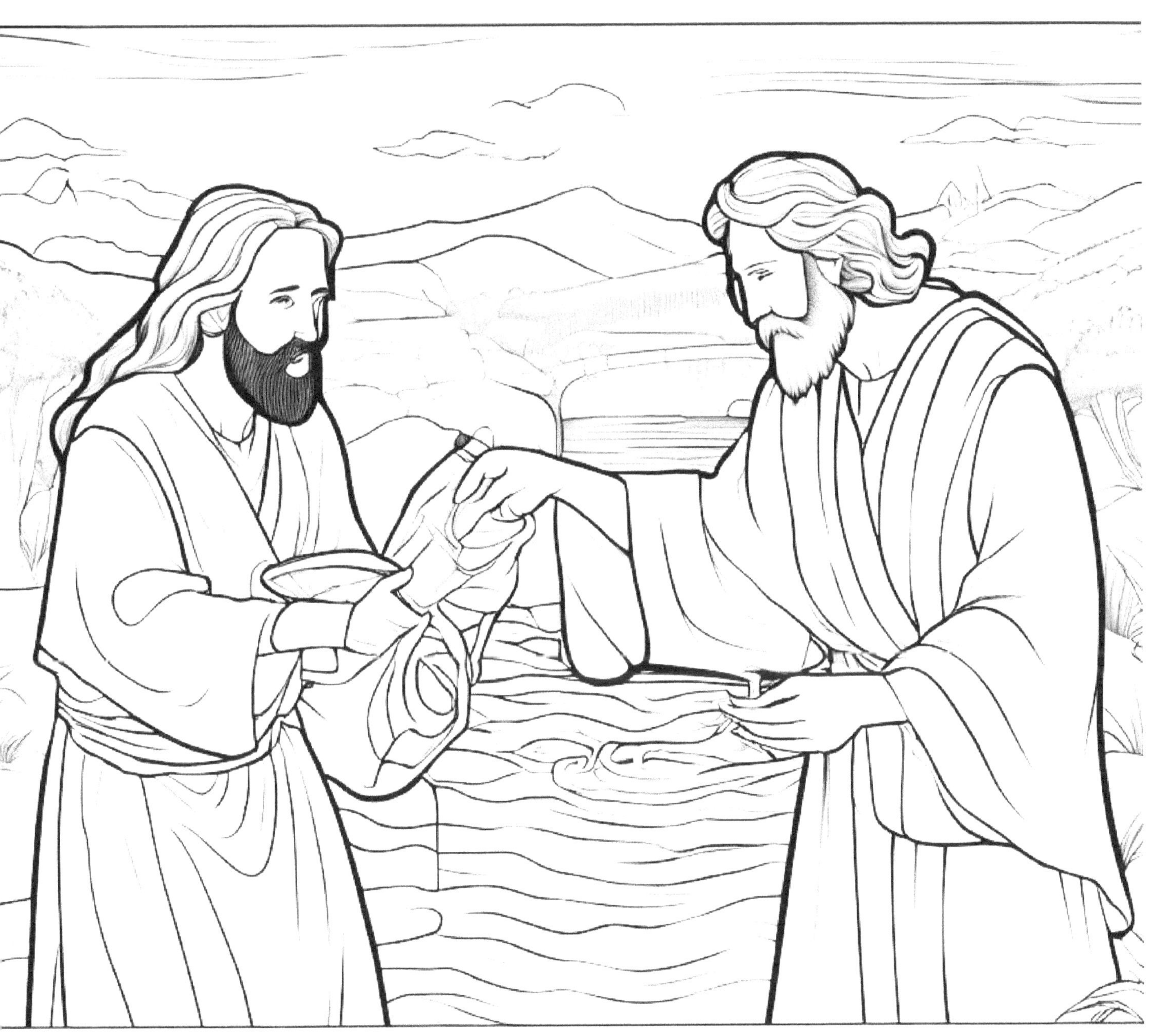

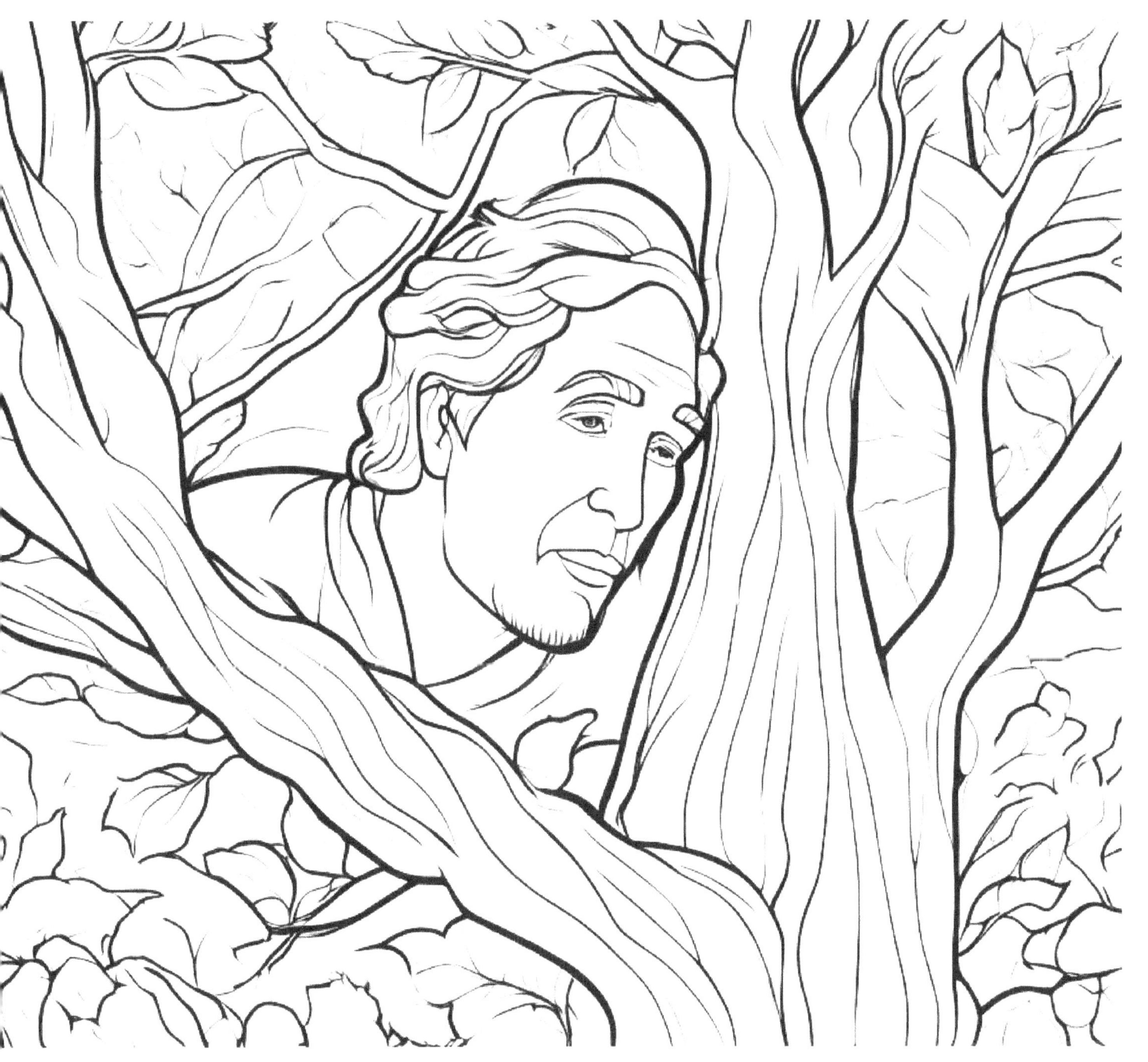

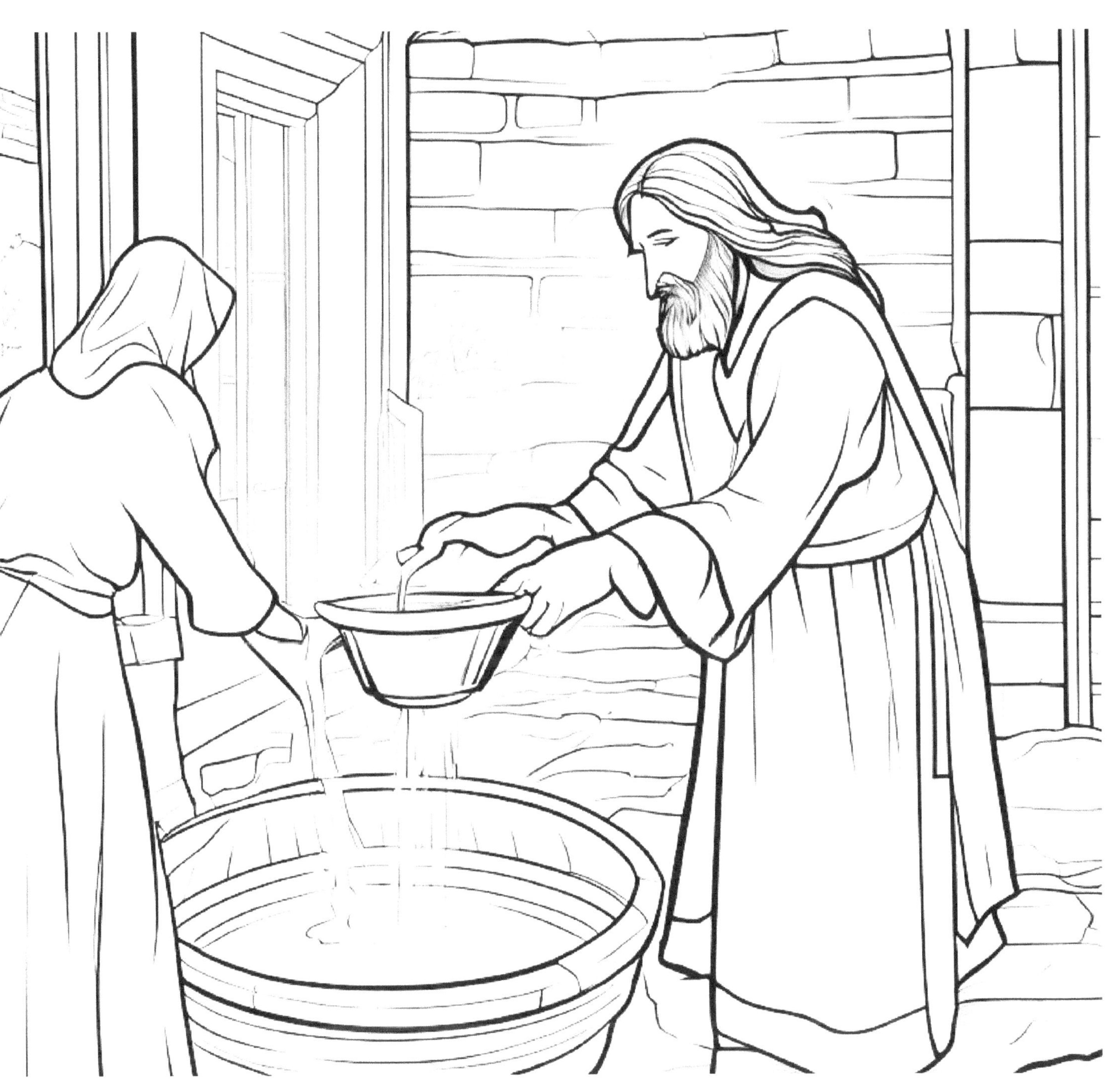

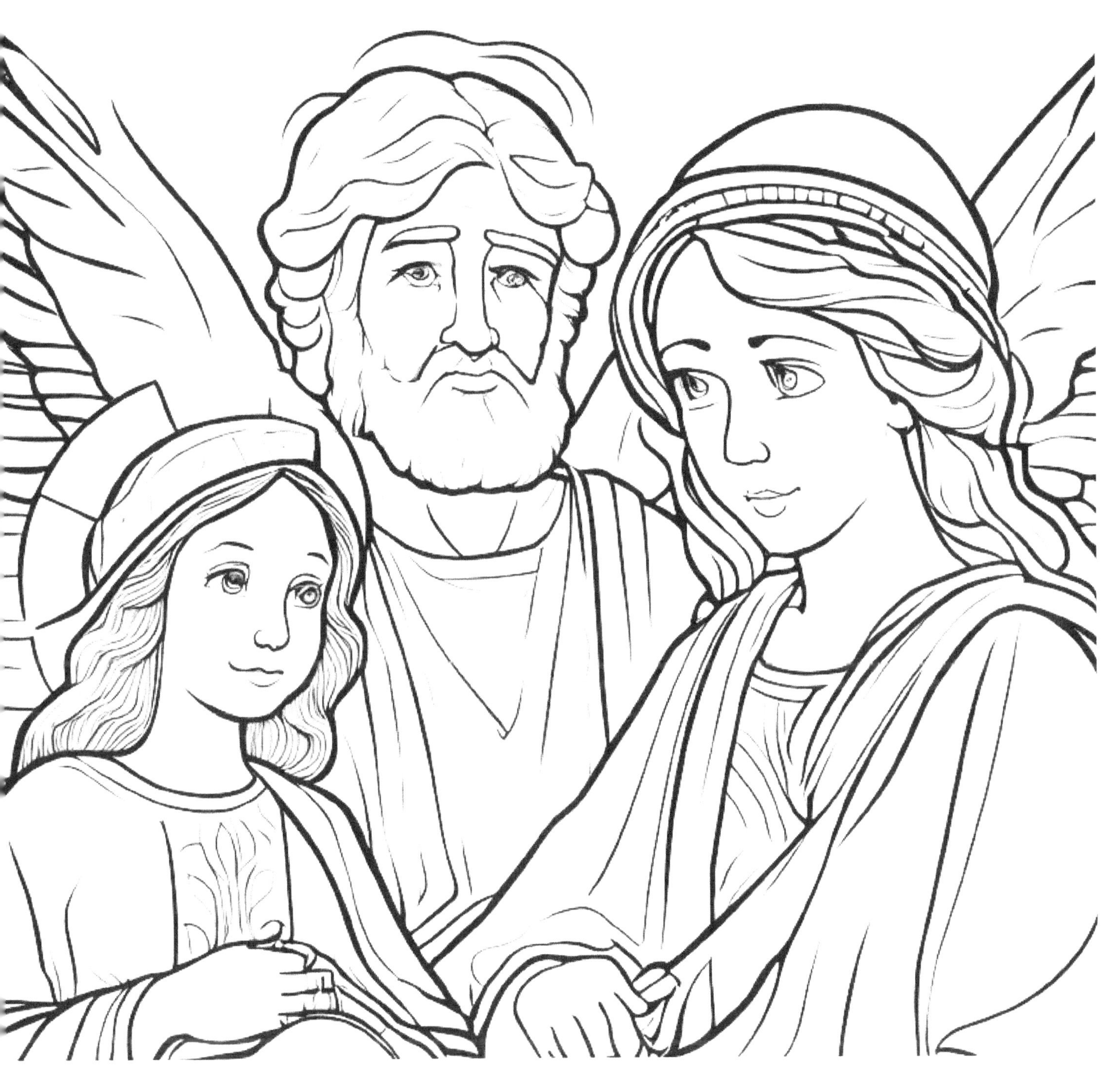

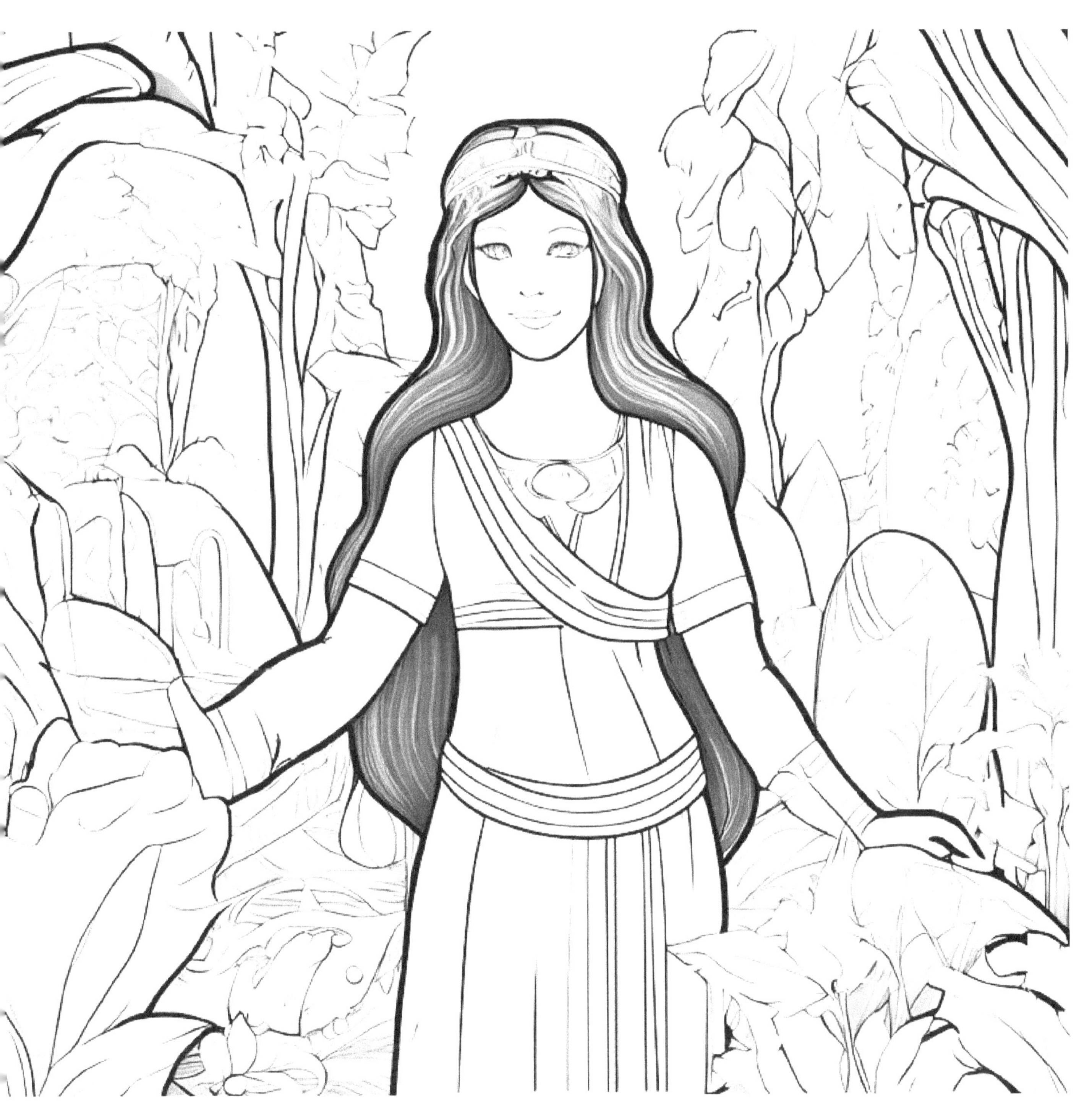

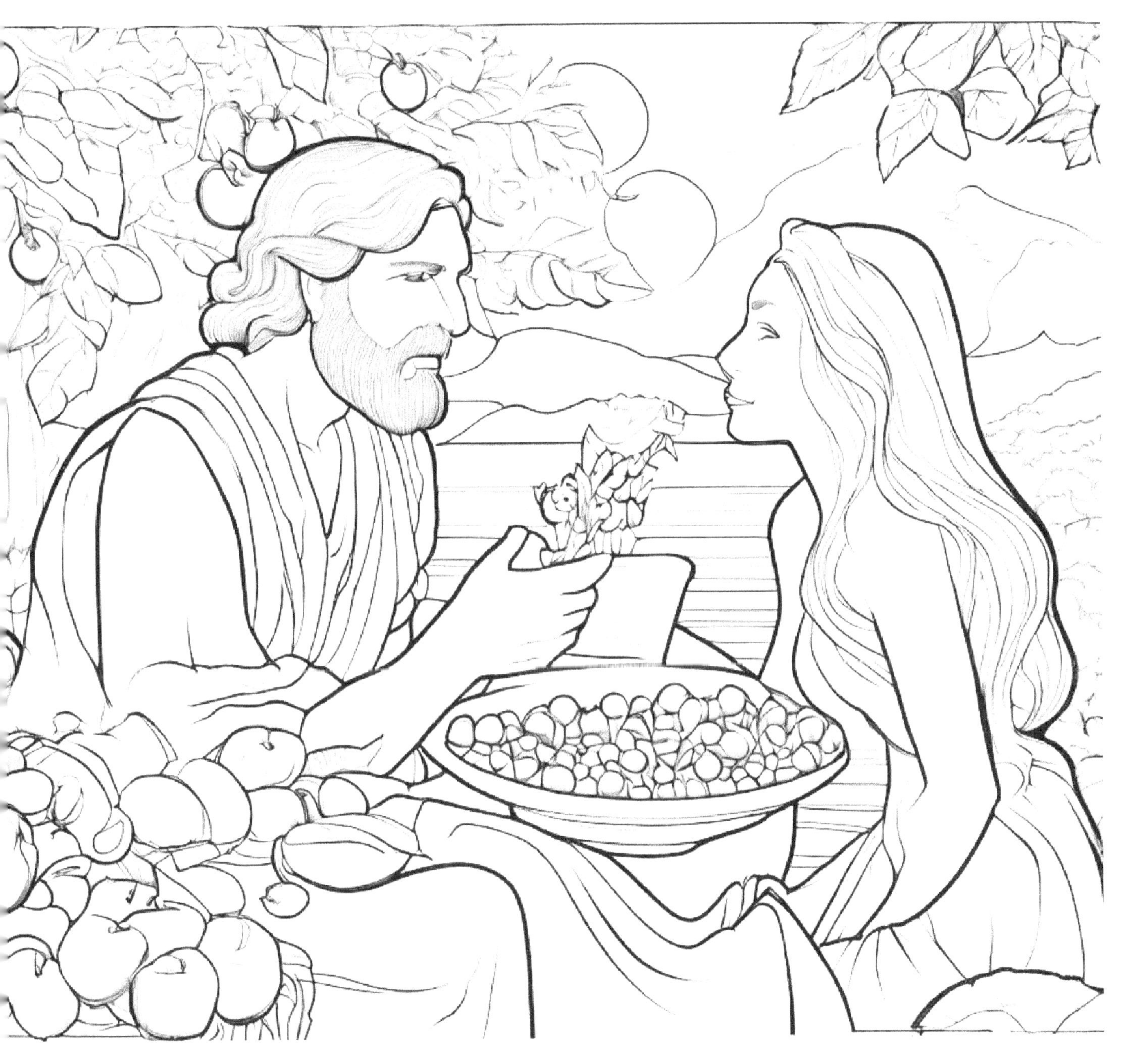

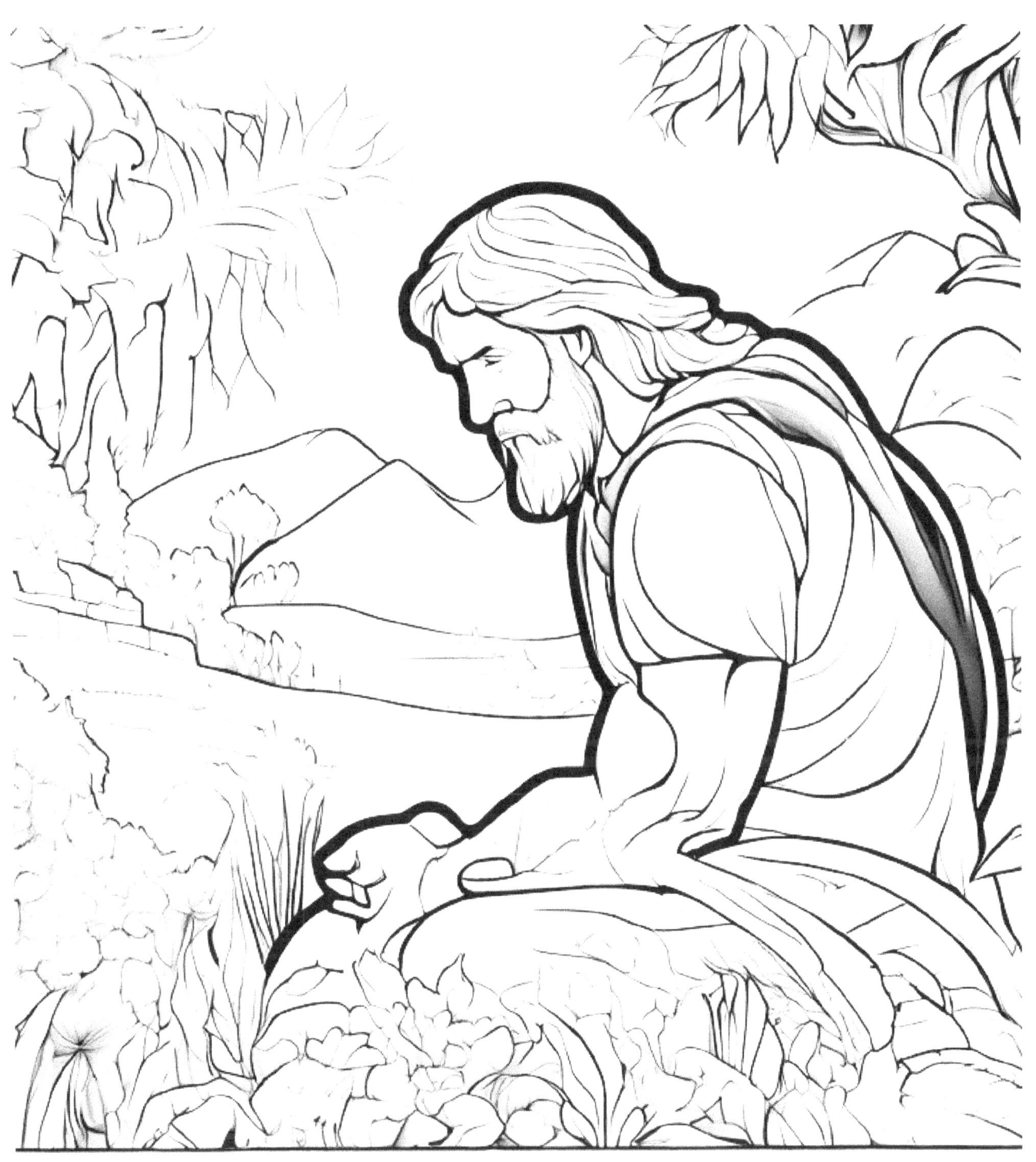

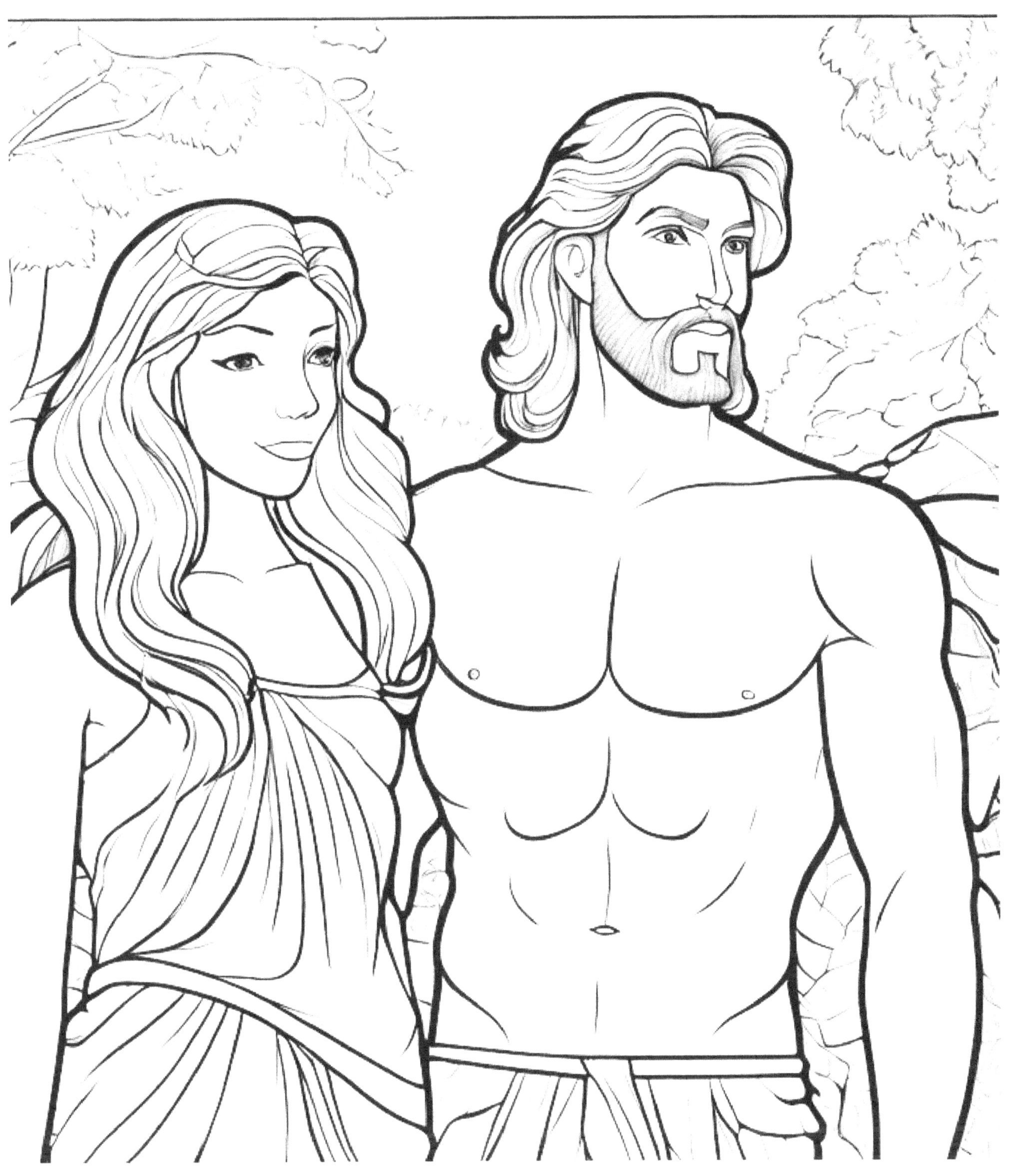

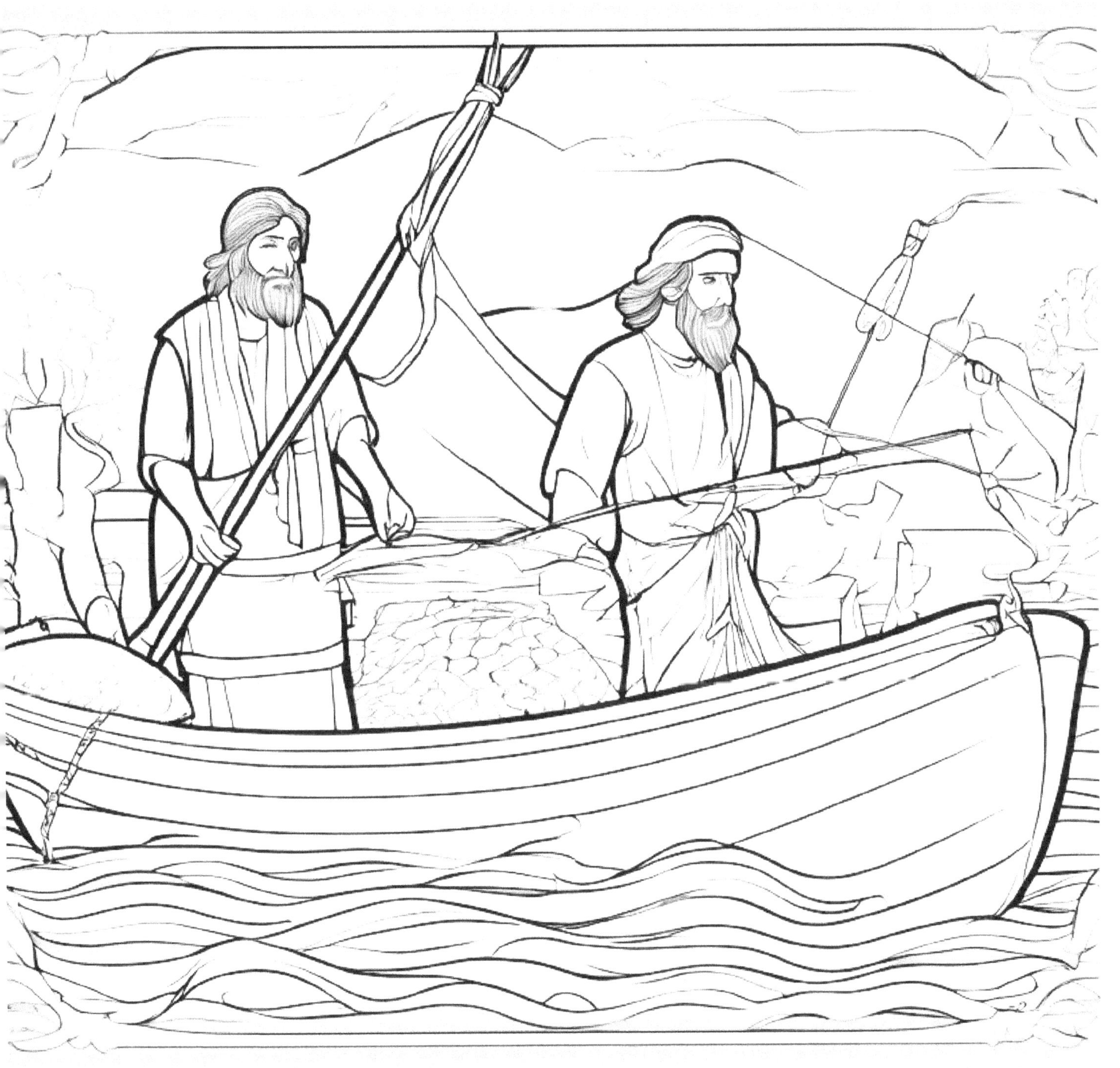

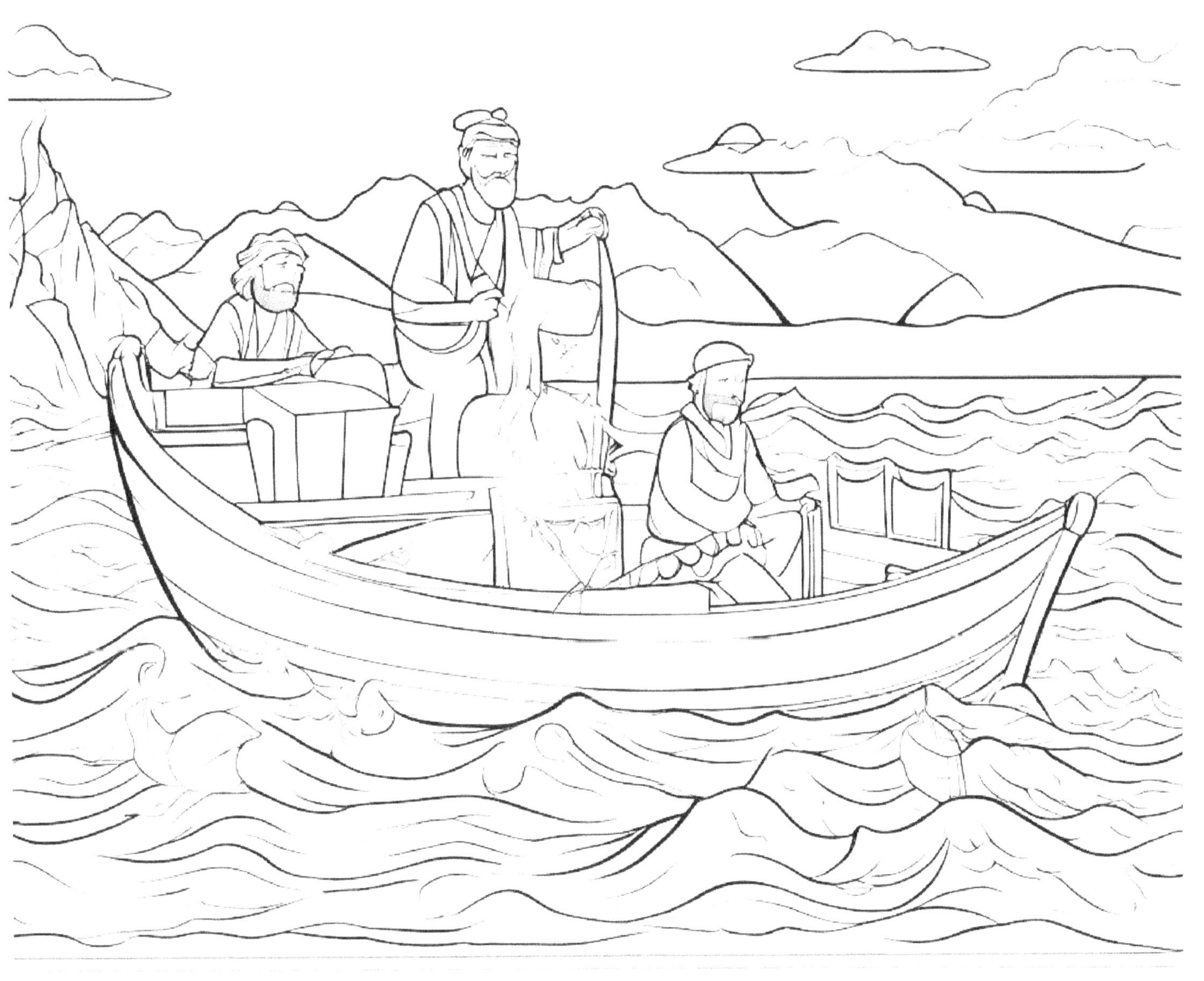

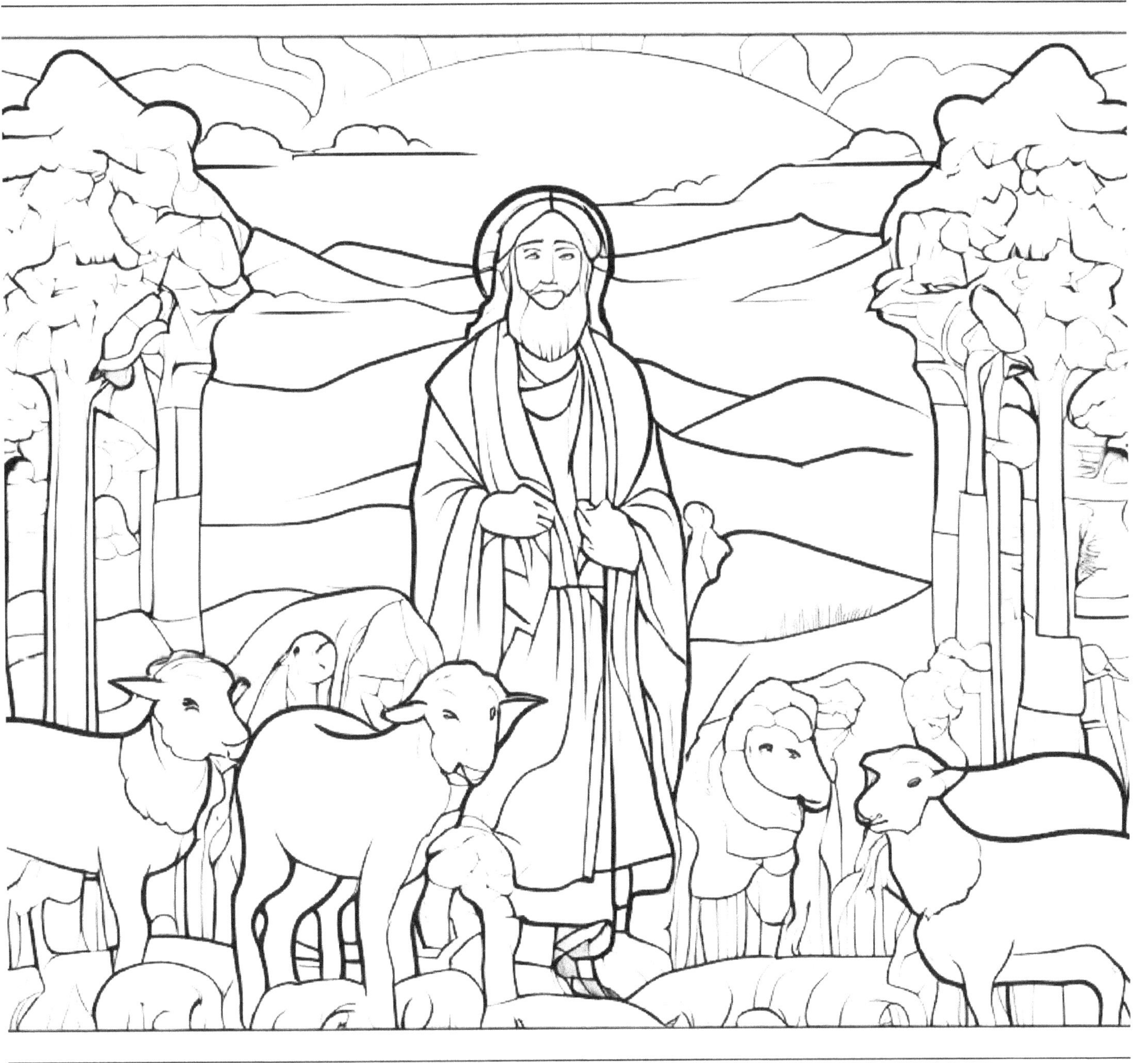

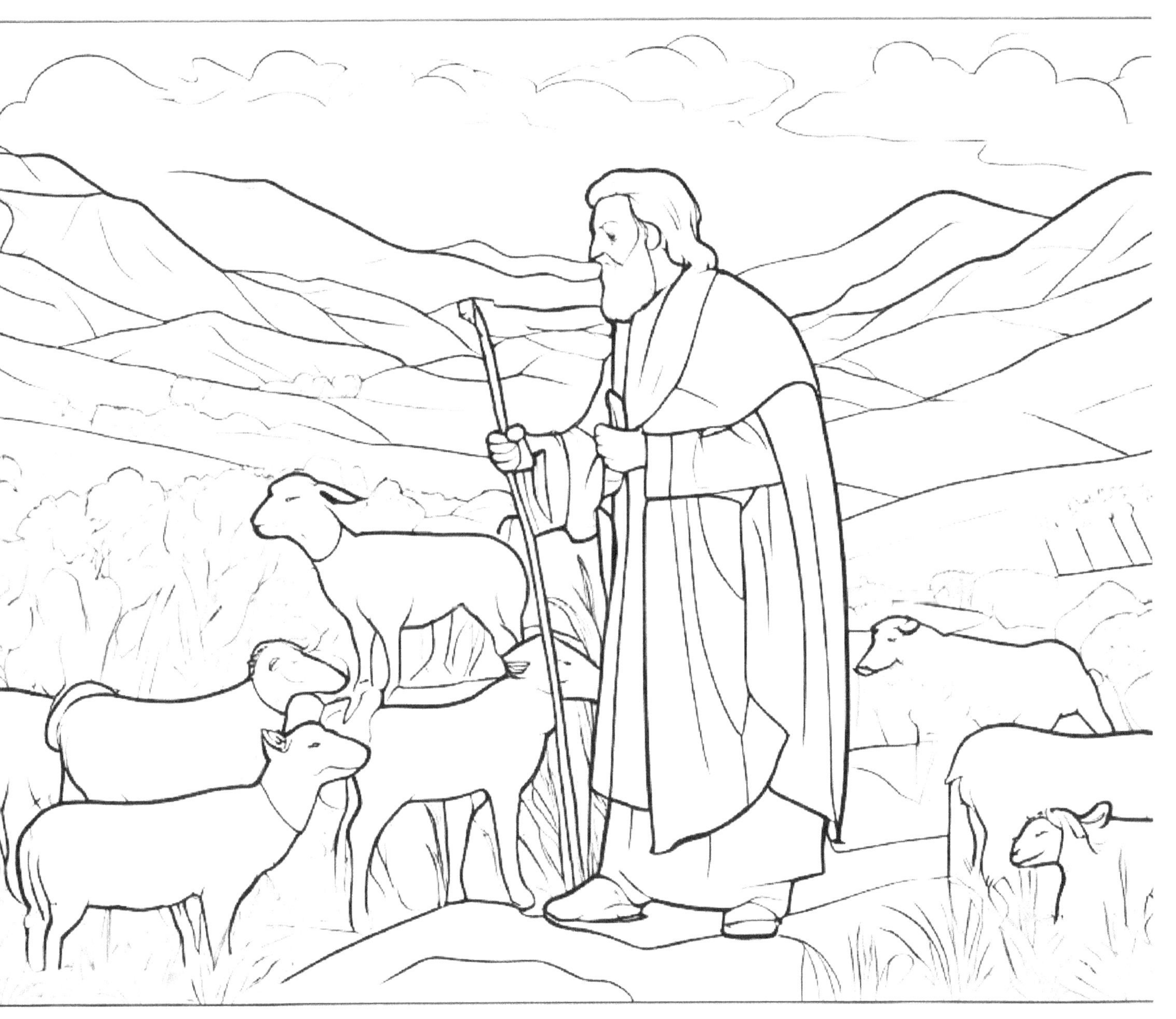

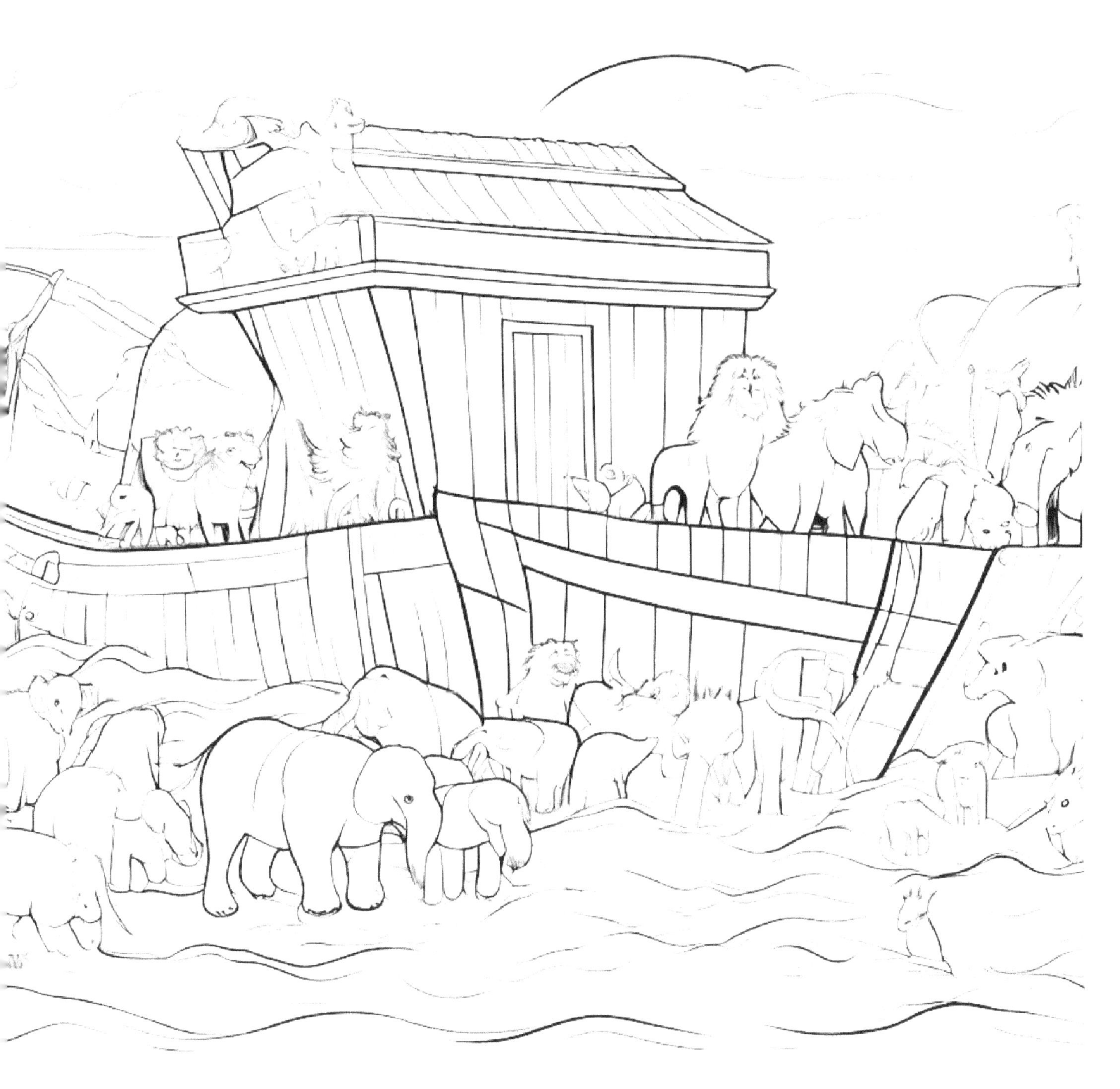

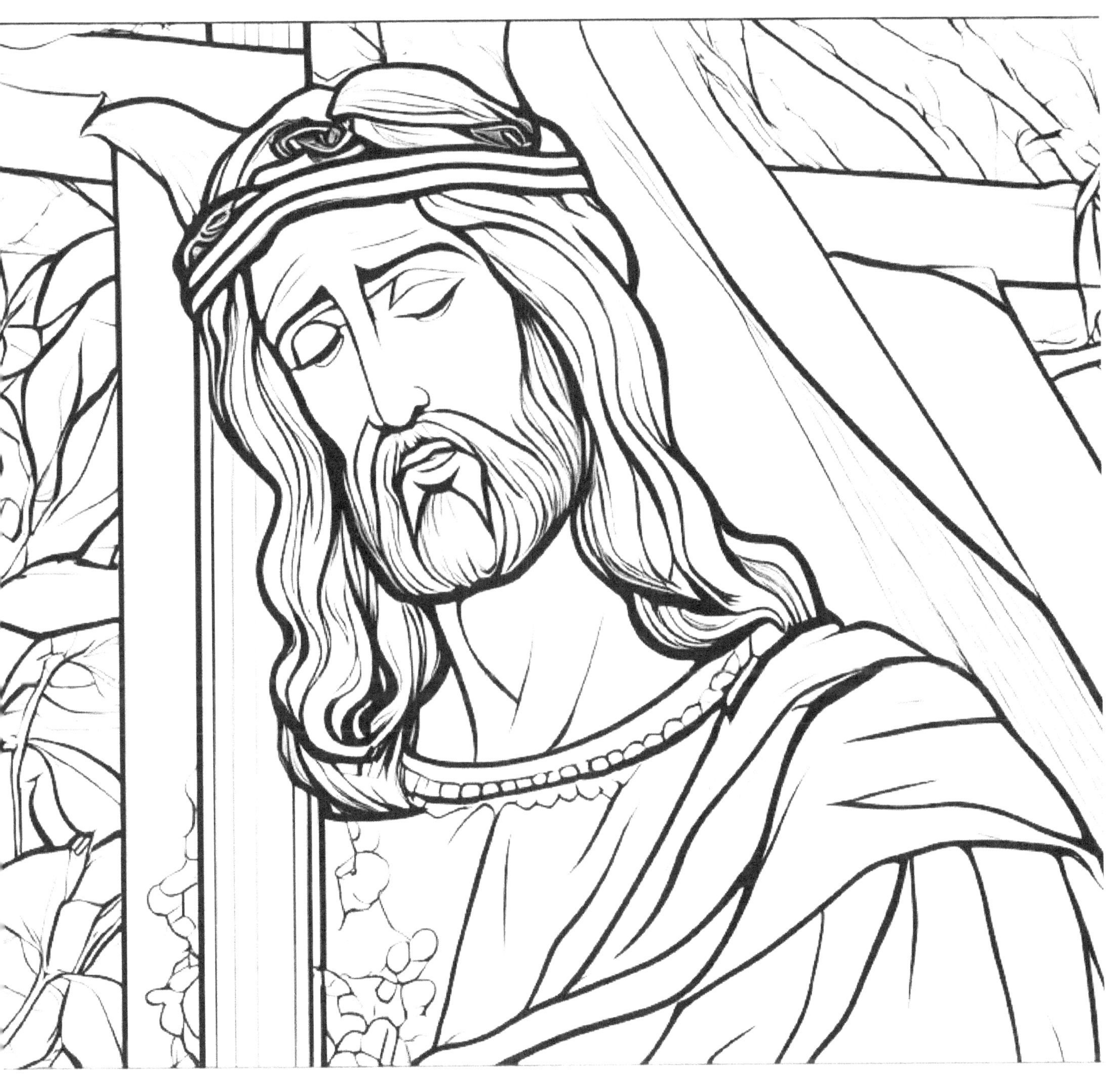

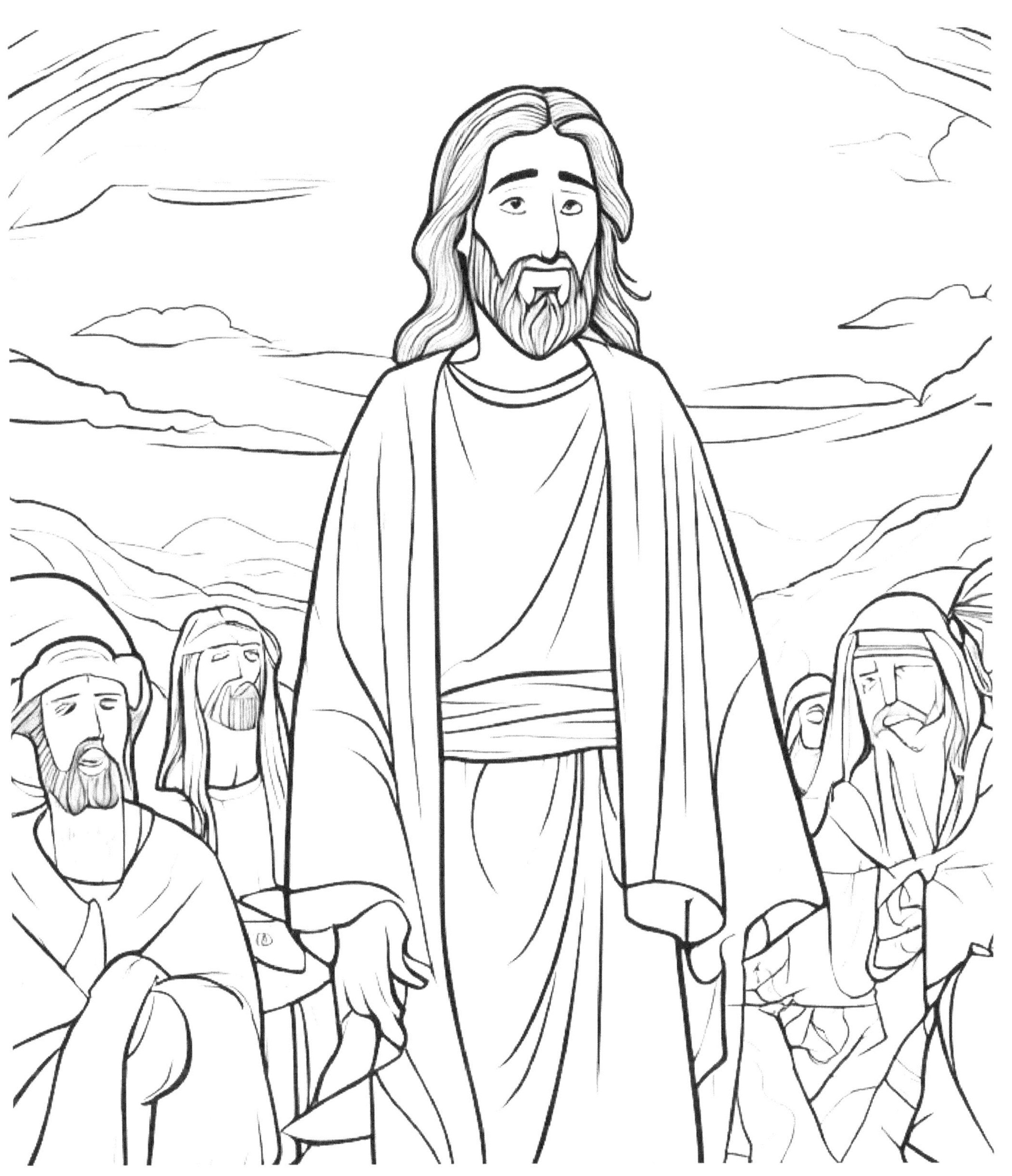

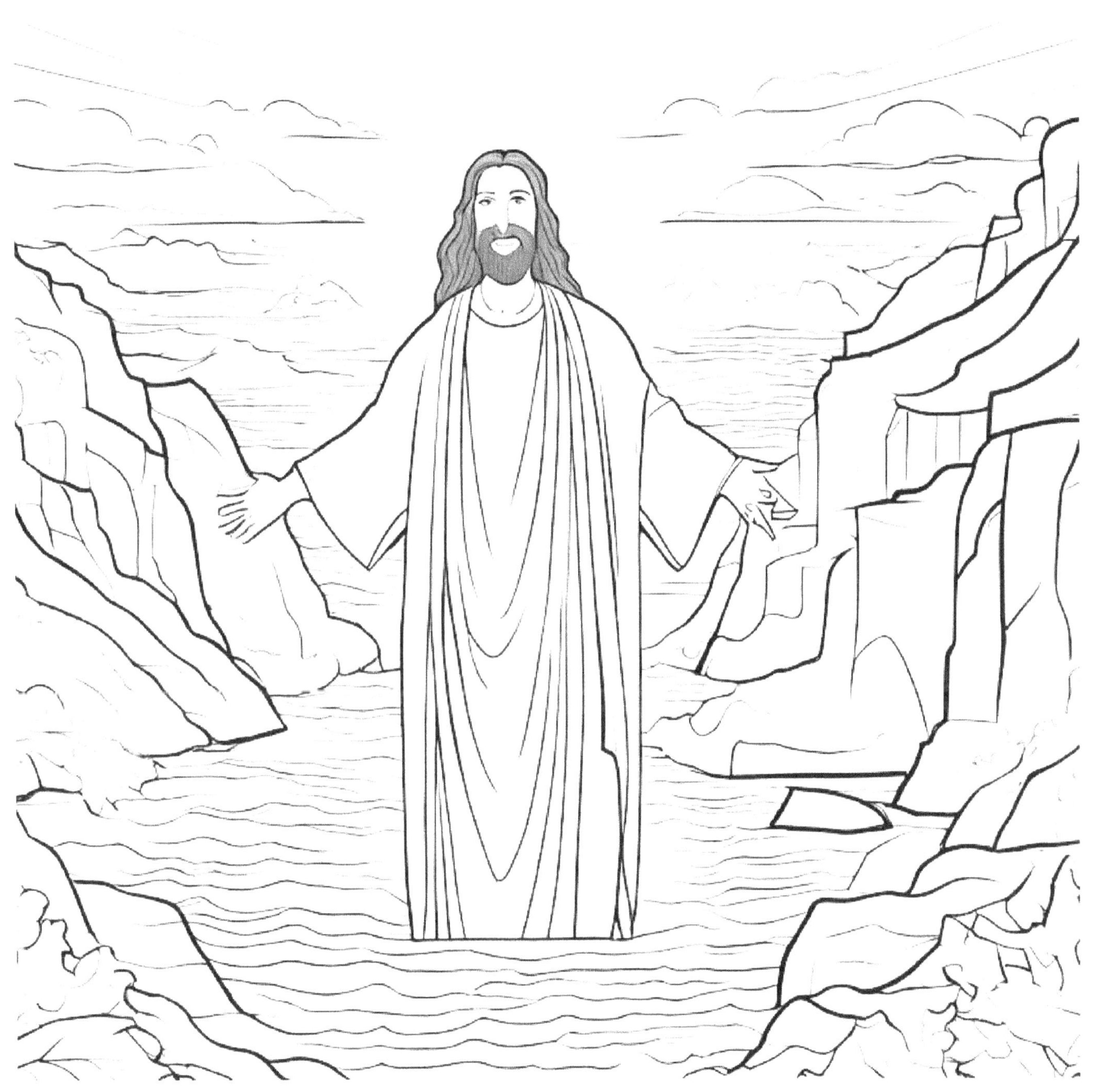

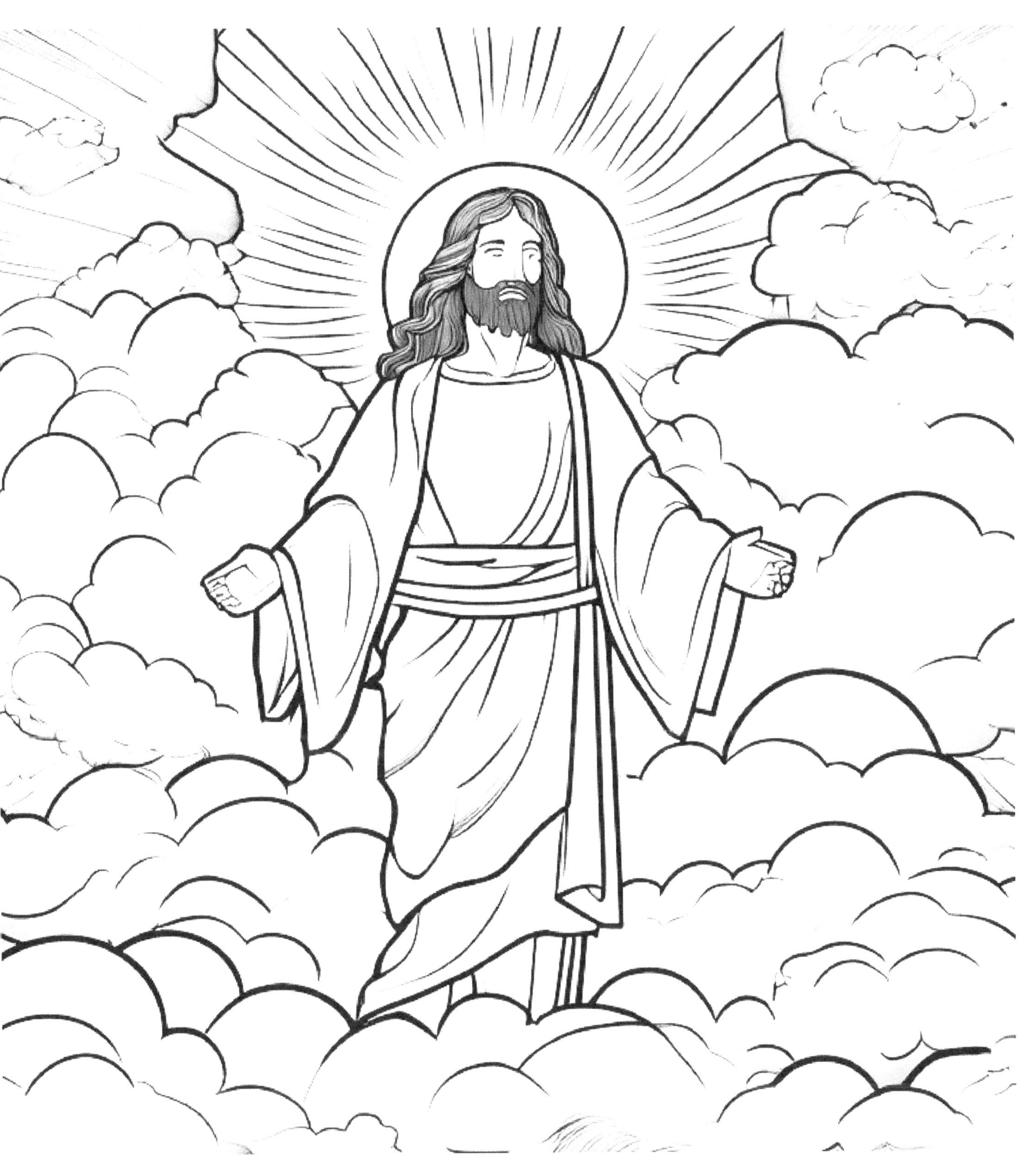

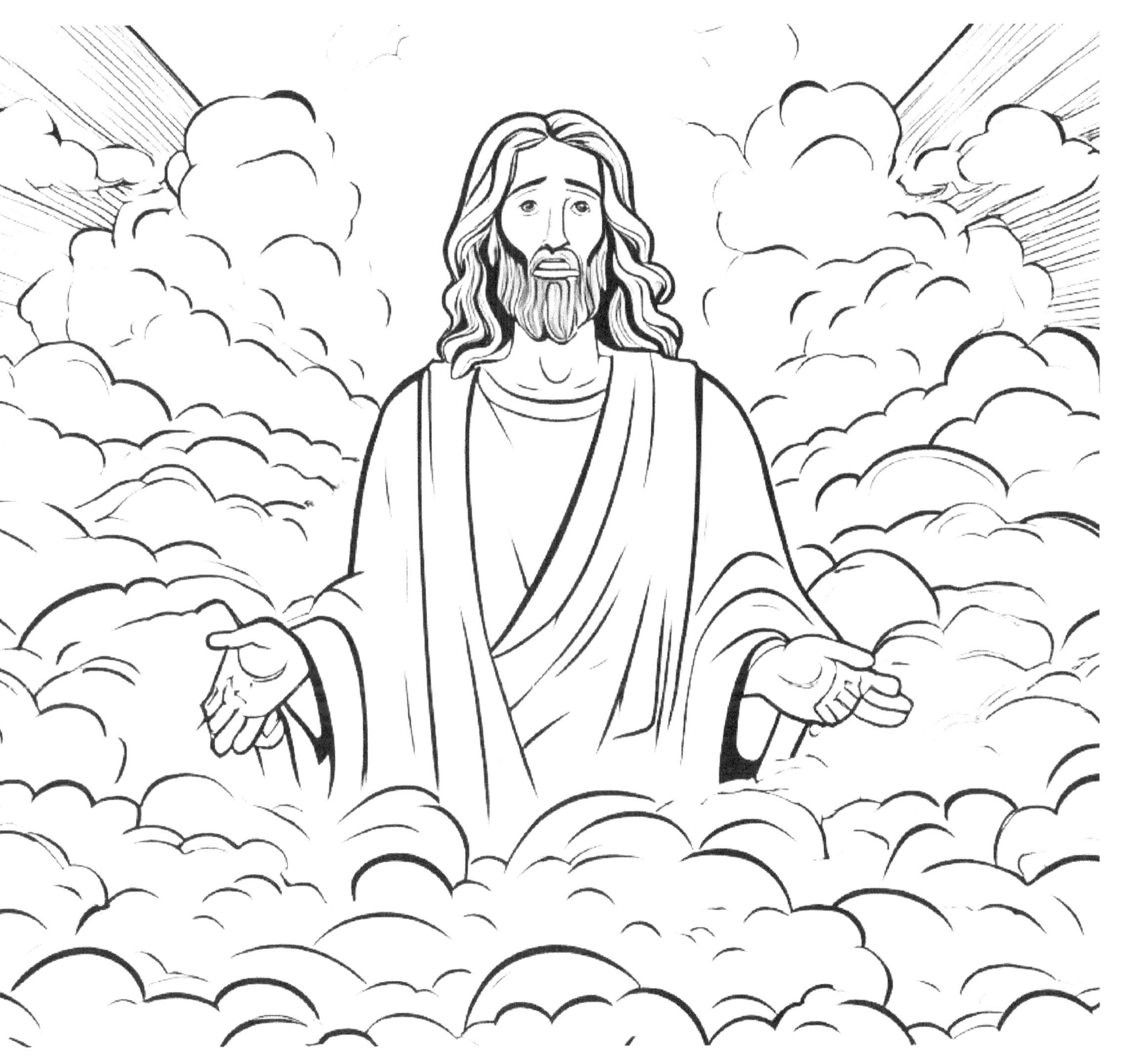